# Counterplot

ALSO BY EDWARD JAY EPSTEIN

INQUEST:
The Warren Commission
and the Establishment of Truth

# Preface

My first book, *Inquest,* began as a master's thesis concerned with the question of establishing the truth
about an event in a charged environment: can the
fact-finding process be insulated from considerations
of anticipated consequences in a matter of political
import? The subject I selected to study was the investigation and report of the President's Commission
on the Assassination of President Kennedy, more generally known as the Warren Commission. Needless to
say, it was a subject that aroused intense emotions
and bitter controversy which at times tended to obscure the issues involved in governmental fact-finding.
It was not, to say the least, a controversy I relished
engaging in for a second time.

The announcement of District Attorney Garrison
that he had uncovered evidence of a conspiracy in
New Orleans was nevertheless of interest to me. In
reading through the Commission's evidence, I had
found a number of unanswered questions about Lee
Harvey Oswald's activities in New Orleans, and I
thought that the New Orleans District Attorney might
throw some light on these unexplored areas in Os-

wald's life. If Garrison had indeed found solid evidence that the murder of President John F. Kennedy was not the work of a lone assassin, as the Warren Commission had concluded, it would of course tend to confirm my thesis that the Commission's investigation —for both bureaucratic and political reasons—had been superficial. I was also intrigued by the possibility that a local district attorney, presumably not constrained by bureaucratic pressures and political considerations of the kind the Warren Commission had had to cope with, could find relevant evidence that had eluded a body working with the resources of the federal government at its disposal.

William Shawn, the editor of *The New Yorker*, agreed that a comparison of the two investigations might help to clarify some of the problems involved in forensic fact-finding, and, in April 1967, I went to New Orleans to pursue this line of inquiry. After interviewing District Attorney Garrison and most of the members of his staff, and examining some of the elements in his case, I realized that the means by which Garrison was attempting to establish his version of the event as the truth were drastically different from those employed by the Warren Commission. Paradoxically, the Commission, essentially an *ad hoc* body outside the judicial system, had attempted to build its case through a quasi-legal process—involving testimony, corroboration, and evaluation more or less in accordance with the customary rules of evidence—whereas Garrison, a duly constituted legal authority, was attempting to establish his case by appealing directly to public opinion. The manner in which Garrison used the powers of his office and the mass media to affect public opinion came to be the focus of this study.

I am indebted to those members of the press who rendered me assistance in tracking down the many charges and countercharges made in this case, including David L. Chandler, John T. Dunkin, Russell W. Freeburg, Robert Hollingsworth, Rosemary James, Eric Norden, James R. Phelan, Walter Sheridan, James D. Squires, John H. Taylor, and Jack Wardlaw. I owe a special debt to my research assistant Cynthia Worswick, who systematically collected all of the District Attorney's public statements and television transcripts; to Fred Freed, who made available to me material from NBC's investigation of the Garrison inquiry; and to Thomas Bethell and Jones Harris, who kept me abreast of developments in the District Attorney's office.

I would also like to thank Richard N. Billings, Robert Bingham, Marc Green, Andrew and Lois Hacker, Bruce Kovner, David Lifton, Seymour Martin Lipset, Charles McLaughlin, Sylvia Meagher, Paul Weaver, and James Q. Wilson for reading the manuscript and making many valuable suggestions.

Finally, I am deeply grateful to William Shawn for the latitude and editorial help he gave me in writing the article for *The New Yorker*, and to Aaron Asher, my editor at The Viking Press, for encouraging and in many ways assisting me to expand the article into this book.

—Edward Jay Epstein

Cambridge, Massachusetts
December 1968

TO MY PARENTS

# Contents

# COUNTERPLOT

## Edward Jay Epstein

THE VIKING PRESS / NEW YORK

# Counterplot

# Prologue:
# Oswald in New Orleans

On September 28, 1964, the President's Commission on the Assassination of President Kennedy, popularly known as the Warren Commission, issued its formal conclusion that Lee Harvey Oswald, acting alone, was responsible for the murder of John F. Kennedy. In the effort to prove that Oswald had no accomplices in the crime, the Commission attempted to reconstruct as precisely as possible the principal events of Oswald's life. However, despite the availability of diaries which he had kept over the years, as well as other personal effects and documents and the testimony of witnesses who claimed to have known him or known of him, charting the alleged assassin's movements was no easy task. For it was clear to the Commission from the outset that Lee Harvey Oswald was an itinerant, elusive, self-occupied individual. The biography of such a subject was bound to be, at best, a sketchy and imperfect record.

Of all the obscure periods in Oswald's life, few seemed to be potentially more significant, and at the same time more puzzling, than the summer of 1963, just before the assassination; it was then that Oswald again took up residence in his native New Orleans. For the Warren Commission, aspects of that summer in New Orleans seemed especially crucial, since it was during those months that Oswald appeared to have engaged in the sort of murky political activity and intrigue which might suggest a possible motive for the assassination. Although Commission lawyers were able to piece together fragments of Oswald's stay in New Orleans, it was evident, when their Report was published, that important gaps remained in the narrative, gaps which the Commission had not succeeded in filling in.

That fragmentary account of the New Orleans interval begins on April 25, 1963, when Oswald stepped off the night bus from Dallas. He carried with him two duffel bags, containing clothes and a few other personal belongings, including a Mannlicher-Carcano rifle which had been purchased a month before from a mail-order house in Chicago. His wife, Marina, testified that the rifle was partly responsible for Oswald's going to New Orleans. "I wanted to get him further removed from Dallas and from [Major General] Walker," she explained to the Warren Commission, "because a rifle for him was a toy that was too enticing."[1] Oswald, however, told a friend that he decided to move because "New Orleans is my home; I like the high ceilings and the trees and the French Quarter, and everything about New Orleans."[2]

From the bus depot, Oswald telephoned Lillian Murret, an aunt whom he hadn't seen since he was a child. Mrs. Murret recalled that she was surprised to hear from her nephew—the last news she had had of him was when he defected to Russia in 1959—and that she invited Oswald to stay with her family while he looked for a job in New Orleans. During the three weeks he lived with them, Mrs. Murret testified, Oswald said very little about his travels or plans for the future. He spent the days job-hunting, and in the evenings seemed concerned about tracing his own past. He went to Lakeview Cemetery to locate the grave of his father, who had died two months before he was born. And he methodically went down the list of Oswalds in the New Orleans telephone directory, calling each of them until he found the only one who was related to him—his uncle's widow, Mrs. Hazel Oswald. She gave him a framed photograph of his father (which he later apparently discarded).[3]

On May 9, he finally managed to find a job. Responding to a newspaper advertisement, Oswald was hired as a greaser and oiler of coffee-processing machinery at the William B. Reily Company. He rented a furnished apartment on Magazine Street, which parallels the industrial canal, for sixty-five dollars a month. He then called Marina, whom he had married

in Russia and brought back to America with him from
Minsk, and said he was ready for her to come to New
Orleans.

Ruth Paine, the Russian-speaking woman with
whom Marina was staying in Dallas, recalled how
excited Marina was at hearing from Lee: *"Papa nas
lubet,"* "Daddy loves us," she repeated over and
over to June, their fourteen-month-old daughter. The
next day, Mrs. Paine drove Marina and June to New
Orleans. Oswald, she told the Commission, was quite
proud of the apartment he had chosen: "He was
pleased there was room enough. . . . And he pointed
out this little courtyard with grass, and fresh straw-
berries ready to pick, where June could play. . . . And
he was pleased with the furniture and how the land-
lady had said this was early New Orleans style."
But Marina was less enthusiastic. "It is dark, and it
is not very clean," she said; and she noticed the cock-
roaches.[4]

Nonetheless, the first few weeks in New Orleans
seemed to Marina a pleasant change from Dallas. Oswald took his family for outings to the beaches,
parks, and zoo. On weekends they would tour the
French Quarter or go to the shores of Lake Pontchartrain where, as Marina put it, "Lee liked to go and
hunt crabs." Oswald told his wife that he was doing
"photographic work" (although he actually spent his
days greasing coffee machines). In the evening he
read books—*Portrait of a Revolutionary: Mao Tse-
tung* by Robert Payne, *Portrait of a President* by William Manchester, *The Huey Long Murder Case* by
Hermann B. Deutsch—borrowed from the neighbor-

hood branch of the public library. Or he pursued his losing battle with the roaches—"He was always in the back of the house, spraying," his landlord observed.[5]

But near the end of May, things changed. Marina wrote to her friend Ruth Paine, "I am very hurt that Lee's attitude towards me is such that I feel each minute that I bind him."[6] Lee had told her that he felt "lost" in America and wanted to return to Russia with her and June. Marina wanted to stay, but her husband insisted that she write to the Soviet Embassy in Washington, to request repatriation. As the summer progressed, he seemed increasingly concerned with sending his family to Russia, and in July he had Marina write a second letter asking the Embassy to rush their visas. Without telling her, Oswald added a note to the letter, asking that his application for a visa be considered "separately" from that of his wife and child. He apparently had plans of his own.[7]

Oswald also seemed to be worried about the "undesirable" discharge he had received from the Marine Corps, and consulted a New Orleans lawyer, Dean Adams Andrews, Jr., about the possibility of having it converted to an honorable discharge. Oswald returned to the lawyer's office at least two more times, accompanied by a stocky, well-built Mexican. Andrews also told the Warren Commission that he later assumed Oswald had been sent to his office by one Clay Bertrand—"mostly a voice on a phone," as Andrews described him, who occasionally had called him to obtain bond or parole for "gay kids"—because, he said, it was Bertrand who phoned him after the assassination to suggest that he defend Oswald in Dallas.[8] The Warren

Commission, however, was not able to find any trace
of Clay Bertrand or of the Mexican.

By mid-July, Oswald had been fired from his job at
the Reily coffee company. Although Marina vaguely
knew that her husband was engaged in some sort of
"pro-Cuban" project, she had little idea of exactly
how he spent his last seventy-odd days in New Orleans.
Oswald, however, summarized his pro-Castro activities
in a brief autobiographical sketch:

> On May 29, 1963, I requested permission from the
> FPCC [Fair Play for Cuba Committee] headquarters
> at 799 Broadway, New York 3, N.Y., to try to form a
> local branch in New Orleans. I received a cautious
> but enthusiastic go-ahead from V. T. Lee, National
> Director of FPCC. I then made layouts and had printed
> public literature for the setting up of a local FPCC. I
> hired persons to distribute literature. I then organized
> persons who display receptive attitudes towards Cuba
> to distribute pamphlets.
>
> I sought response from Latin American consuls of
> which there are many here in New Orleans. I infil-
> trated the Cuban Student Directorate and then har-
> assed them with information I gained, including having
> the New Orleans city attorney general call them and
> put a restraining order pending a hearing on some so-
> called bonds for an invasion they were selling in the
> New Orleans area. I caused the formation of a small,
> active FPCC organization of members and sympa-
> thizers where before there was none.
>
> I am experienced in street agitation having done it in
> New Orleans in connection with the FPCC. On August
> 9, 1963, I was accosted by three anti-Castro Cubans
> and was arrested for "causing a disturbance." I was

interrogated by intelligence section of New Orleans Police Department and held overnight, being bailed out the next morning by relatives. I subsequently was fined $10; charges against the three Cubans were dropped by the judge.

On August 16 I organized a four-man FPCC demonstration in front of the International Trade Mart in New Orleans. This demonstration was filmed by WDSU-TV and shown on the 6:00 news.

On August 17 I was invited by WDSU-Radio to appear on the August 17 radio program Latin American Focus at 7:30 p.m. The moderator was Bill Stucky, who put questions to me for a half an hour about FPCC attitudes and opinions.

After this program I was invited to take part in a radio debate between John [Edward S.] Butler of INCA, anti-Communist propaganda representative, and Carlos Bringuier, Cuban exile Student Revolutionary Directorate delegate in New Orleans. This debate was broadcast at 6:05 to 6:30 August 21, 1963; after this program I made a three-minute TV newsreel which was shown the next day (August 22).

I received advice, direction and literature from V. T. Lee, National Director of the Fair Play for Cuba Committee, of which I am a member. At my own expense I had printed "Hands Off Cuba" handbills and New Orleans branch membership blanks for the FPCC local.[9]

Although this résumé was documented with newspaper clippings, letters from the Fair Play for Cuba Committee and the Communist Party, subscription receipts from the *Worker* and from Soviet journals, membership cards in the FPCC, etc., it was neither totally accurate nor candid. For one thing, the "FPCC organization" which Oswald said he formed in New Orleans had never been authorized by the FPCC; in fact, it didn't even exist. While it is true that Oswald wrote to the Fair Play for Cuba Committee in New York, requesting a "charter" for a New Orleans chapter and a "picture of Fidel, suitable for framing," and offered to rent an office at his own expense, the reply he received was hardly encouraging. V. T. Lee, the national director of the FPCC, wrote Oswald that a charter for a New Orleans chapter could not be granted until a requisite number of members had been duly enrolled, and V. T. Lee expressed doubt that Oswald would find sufficient members in the New Orleans area. Moreover, he specifically asked Oswald not to rent an office.

A few days later, Oswald wrote another letter to V. T. Lee. "Against your advice," he told the national director, "I have decided to take an office."[10] Whether or not Oswald actually did rent an office, however, is a moot point. The cachet "FPCC, 544 CAMP ST." appears on some of the pro-Castro literature Oswald possessed, but the building at 544 Camp Street, which was a block from the coffee company where Oswald had worked, housed an *anti*-Castro group known as the Cuban Revolutionary Council. W. Guy Banister, a New Orleans private detective heavily involved in anti-Castro activities, also maintained offices in that building, and one of Banister's investigators, Jack S. Martin, had helped set up the Cuban Revolutionary Council at that address.[11] After the assassination, it was Jack Martin who alleged that David William Ferrie, for a short time also a New Orleans private detective, was to have been Oswald's "getaway pilot," but later he recanted this story.[12]

In his second letter to V. T. Lee, Oswald also enclosed a circular that read: "HANDS OFF CUBA! JOIN THE FAIR PLAY FOR CUBA COMMITTEE. NEW ORLEANS CHARTER MEMBER BRANCH. FREE LITERATURE, LECTURES, EVERYONE WELCOME." And he added, "As you see from the circular I had jumped the gun on the charter business, but I don't think it's too important."[13] (Using the alias Lee Osborne, Oswald had had two thousand such circulars printed.) Finally, Oswald said that he had decided on a "major change of tactics" for his "chapter."

V. T. Lee did not reply to this or to any of the subsequent letters Oswald sent to the FPCC. He testified before the Warren Commission that he had been quite disturbed that Oswald "had gone ahead and acted on his own without any authorization from the organization" and had violated the "rules of the organization" by setting up a "chapter" under the "name of the organization."[14]

Moreover, Oswald's "FPCC chapter" apparently had only one member: Oswald. Marina testified that her husband had forced her to sign the name "A. J. Hidell, Chapter President"* on the FPCC membership card he had had printed (under still another alias), explaining to her that it was necessary to use a fictitious name so that "people will think I have a big organization."[15] Marina

---

* Oswald also used the alias "Hidell" on three other occasions: on a vaccination certificate, as an employment reference, and on the order blank for the Mannlicher-Carcano rifle.

recalled that when a Cuban man had come to their apartment to make inquiries about joining Oswald's FPCC chapter, her husband made no effort to enroll him; he subsequently explained to her that the caller was probably "some anti-Castro Cuban or perhaps an FBI agent."[16] Oswald, it turned out, was right: the inquirer, Carlos Quiroga, a prominent anti-Castro exile leader, later told Secret Service investigators that he had been trying to "infiltrate Oswald's organization."[17] Marina was certain that no one ever joined what she called Oswald's "non-existing organization."[18]

Oswald's description of the "demonstrations" was also somewhat hyperbolic. After single-handedly picketing the aircraft carrier U.S.S. *Wasp* (until he was unceremoniously expelled from the pier by a patrolman), he wrote V. T. Lee, "We managed to picket the fleet when it came in and I was surprised at the number of officers who were interested in our literature."[19] While it is true that on August 9, 1963, Oswald did, as he reports, get involved in a fracas with three anti-Castroites, the incident appears to have been planned and provoked by Oswald himself. On August 1, eight days *before* the reported incident took place, Oswald wrote V. T. Lee that a "street demonstration" which he organized was "attacked" by "Cuban-exile gusanos (worms)" and that afterward "we were officially cautioned by the police."[20] This letter was sent on August 4.[21] The next day Oswald visited the Casa Roca, a haberdashery that served as a center for anti-Castro activity. When Oswald entered the store, the manager, Carlos Bringuier, was discussing the sale of ten-dollar Cuban invasion bonds with two teen-agers. Oswald casually introduced himself to Bringuier, who claimed to be the New Orleans representative of the Cuban Student Directorate, and told him that he had been trained in guerrilla warfare in the Marine Corps and now wanted to "train Cubans to fight against Castro." To prove his mettle, Oswald furnished some on-the-spot suggestions for blowing up the Huey P. Long bridge ("put powder charges at each end of the bridge from the foundation to where the foundation meets the suspension part"); for derailing trains ("put a chain around the railroad track and lock it to the track"); for making zipguns ("tubing and plunger"); and for making gunpowder ("saltpeter and nitrate").[22] Bringuier, however, held Oswald's motives suspect for at least two reasons: after his group had taken part in a shelling of Havana, he had been warned by an FBI agent that the FBI intended to infiltrate his organization; and only a few days before, Bringuier had received word that a pro-Castro agent was attempting to infiltrate the anti-Castro training camps on Lake Pontchartrain. Uncertain as to which side Oswald was really on, Bringuier even refused to accept a cash contribution from him. Oswald returned the next day to leave his Marine training manual with Bringuier.[23]

Then, on August 9, Oswald again appeared in the vicinity of Bringuier's store. This time, he bore a "Viva Fidel" placard and distributed *pro*-Castro propaganda. With a few other Cuban counterrevolutionists, Bringuier rushed out of his store and began shouting at Oswald. "O.K., Carlos," Oswald calmly said, "if you want to hit me, hit me," but Bringuier refused. At this point, the police arrived and arrested both Oswald and Bringuier.[24]

Oswald was, as he said, "interrogated" by the New Orleans police, but he himself volunteered a good deal of information concerning his phantom FPCC chapter. He said he had been associated with the FPCC since 1959; that there were thirty-five members in his FPCC chapter; that they rotated their meetings among various members' homes; and that A. J. Hidell was president of the group.[25] Oswald then *asked* to see an FBI agent. And when an agent, John Lester Quigly, visited Oswald in jail later that day, Oswald tried to convince him that the FPCC was an active, operative group in New Orleans. But the FBI man came away with the impression that Oswald's admissions were false and merely intended as a "self-serving statement."[26] After spending the night in jail, Oswald was released on ten dollars bail.

According to the Warren Commission, Oswald staged his second "demonstration" on August 16. At the Louisiana State Employment office, Oswald hired the sixteen-year-old son of a local deputy sheriff and a second unidentified individual to assist him in distributing "Hands Off Cuba" leaflets in front of the International Trade Mart. (In Oswald's description, it was a "four-man . . . demonstration.") Crews from two local television stations, apparently tipped off in advance, were standing by to capture on TV tape the pro-Castro activities of Lee Harvey Oswald. He wrote V. T. Lee that this demonstration "was given considerable coverage by WDSU-TV channel 6, and also by our channel 4 T.V. station."[27]

A few days after the demonstration, in an interview with reporter William Stuckey on the "Latin Listening Post" radio program, Oswald freely discussed the role of the FPCC in New Orleans—"to attract new members and feel out the public."[28] Next, Stuckey arranged a live radio debate between Oswald, Carlos Bringuier, and Edward S. Butler, the executive vice-president of an organization known as INCA, which specialized "in distributing anti-Communist educational material in Latin America." Oswald was grilled on his pro-Castro activities, and admitted that he was a "Marxist" who had resided in the Soviet Union for three years.[29] After the program, Oswald obligingly made a three-minute TV tape which was broadcast the following day; he carefully mentions these FPCC-related activities in his notes.

William Stuckey, the moderator of the debate, believed that Oswald's public admissions "finished" the FPCC in New Orleans.[30] But Oswald took a more optimistic view. In a letter to V. T. Lee, he reported, "I was flooded with callers and invitations to debate . . . as well as people interested in joining the FPCC New Orleans branch."[31] In a subsequent letter to the Communist Party, to whose top leaders he had already sent "honorary membership cards" in his "chapter," he expressed the fear that he "may have compromised the FPCC," and asked, "Whether in your opinion I should always remain in the background, i.e., underground."[32]

But Oswald seems to have had little intention of going "underground." His autobiographical sketch was prepared for the express purpose of convincing the Cubans that he was a true friend of Castro's revolution. Marina, in fact, viewed all the activities described in the document—the "FPCC chapter," the demonstrations, the publicity—as mere "window dressing" for her husband's real purpose: getting to Cuba.[33] "He wanted to be arrested," she testified, "he wanted to get into the newspapers, so that he would be known" as pro-Cuban. The FPCC operation was, according to Marina, merely "self-advertising."[34]

In September 1963, Oswald began reviewing his Spanish, doing physical exercises, and practicing "dry firing" his rifle almost every night. Marina thought that these preparations were all related to his impending Cuban trip.[35] He also spent considerable time studying world maps and airline schedules; he explained to Marina that he might have to "kidnap an aircraft" and force the pilot to fly him to Cuba.[36]

Oswald eventually adopted another plan. On September 17, he obtained a Tourist Card, under the name "Lee, Harvey Oswald," from the Mexican consulate general in New Orleans; this would permit him to stay in Mexico for fifteen days. Then, on September 24, his sent his wife and daughter back to Dallas with Ruth Paine (after swearing her to silence about the Mexican trip). The next day, he departed.

The Warren Commission was not able to determine exactly how Oswald traveled from New Orleans to Mexico City. One witness, Sylvia Odio, said that Oswald stopped at her house in Dallas on his way to

Mexico, and was accompanied by two "Latins" who identified themselves as members of the anti-Castro underground. The next day, she said, one of the "Latins" called her and said that he wanted to introduce Oswald "to the underground in Cuba, because he is . . . kind of nuts . . . he told us we don't have any guts, you Cubans, because President Kennedy should have been assassinated after the Bay of Pigs."[37] Although the Warren Commission lawyers remained extremely skeptical about Mrs. Odio's story, they were unable to find any real evidence either to confirm or refute it.

In any case, Oswald arrived in Mexico City on September 27, 1963, and checked into the Hotel del Commercio. He went directly to the Cuban Embassy and applied for a visa to Cuba in transit to Russia, representing himself as the "director" of the New Orleans branch of "Fair Play for Cuba" and submitting as proof of his pro-Castro sympathies the documentation he had so carefully gathered during his summer in New Orleans. Returning that afternoon, Oswald was told that the Cuban Embassy could not grant him an in-transit visa before he had obtained a visa from the Soviet Union. On hearing this, Oswald grew "highly agitated and angry," according to an embassy employee, and then became involved in a heated argument with the Cuban consul, who told Oswald that "in place of aiding the Cuban Revolution, [he] was doing it harm." Slamming the door, Oswald left.[38] Later in the week, he was also turned down by the Soviet Embassy. He attributed his failure to obtain visas to "bureaucracy and red tape."[39]

After returning to Dallas in October, Oswald rented a room in a boarding house under the alias O. H. Lee, and then found a job as a stock boy in the Texas School Book Depository, a seven-story building over-looking Dealey Plaza in downtown Dallas.

On November 22, 1963, President John F. Kennedy was shot and killed in Dallas as his motorcade passed through Dealey Plaza. Less than one hour later, Lee Harvey Oswald was arrested and was subsequently charged with the crime. Two days later, Oswald him-self was fatally shot in the basement of the Dallas city jail by Jack Ruby, a Dallas night-club owner. It was ten months later that the Warren Commission, appointed by President Lyndon B. Johnson to ascer-tain the facts, rendered its final verdict that Oswald, acting alone, had assassinated President Kennedy.

# 1

## The First Conspiracy

# The Prosecutor

Arrested this evening in the district attorney's office was Clay Shaw, age 54, of 1313 Dauphine Street, New Orleans, Louisiana. Mr. Shaw will be charged with participating in a conspiracy to murder John F. Kennedy.

—Jim Garrison, March 1, 1967, press release

A great many Americans must have responded with some measure of bewilderment when they heard the news that Jim Garrison, the District Attorney of Orleans Parish, Louisiana, had arrested a prominent New Orleans citizen and the former director of the International Trade Mart, Clay L. Shaw, for participation in a conspiracy to murder John F. Kennedy. The conclusion of the Warren Commission, published some two and a half years before, had offered the authoritative judgment that Lee Harvey Oswald alone was responsible for the assassination. And although a host of doubts were subsequently raised concerning the adequacy of the Warren Commission's investigation and the reliability of its conclusions, it seemed incredible that the New Orleans District Attorney could declare, as Garrison had, "My staff and I solved the assassination weeks ago. I wouldn't say this if we didn't have the evidence beyond a shadow of a doubt."[1] Indeed, the possibility that a local prosecutor had found the answers to questions that had baffled the investigative resources of the federal government seemed so remote to most journalists that, soon after the initial stir provoked by Shaw's arrest, news of the "assassination plot" was generally relegated to the back pages and treated about as seriously as flying-saucer reports.

I, for one, however, was prepared to believe that District Attorney Garrison's claims might have some substance to them. In the course of writing my book *Inquest*,[2] I had found that the Warren Commission's investigation had been severely constrained both by bureaucratic pressures exerted from within and by limits of time imposed from without. Far from being the rigorous and exhaustive examination that it was taken to be, the Commission's work was, at certain crucial points, reduced to little more than an exercise in the clarification of superficial evidence. When one delved more deeply, some far more difficult problems than any acknowledged by the Commission began to appear. Even members of the Commission's own staff found this to be true. For example, when one staff lawyer suggested, late in the investigation, that it might be worthwhile to look further into the partly corroborated story of Sylvia Odio, the witness who had said that Oswald was introduced to her not long before the assassination by two anti-Castro Cubans whom he was traveling with, his superior curtly told him, "At this stage, we are supposed to be closing doors, not opening them."[3] It later turned out that some of the doors left ajar but unopened led to associates of Oswald's in New Orleans, so it seemed entirely conceivable to me that Garrison just might have stumbled upon some valuable information that the Commission had, for one reason or another, sidestepped.

Consider, for example, a story at the root of Garrison's investigation, which involved a meeting among Oswald and three men—David Ferrie, Carlos Quiroga, and W. Guy Banister—all of whom the Warren Commission had had reason to be interested in. Ferrie, who, according to the testimony of one Commission witness, commanded a unit of the Civil Air Patrol in which Oswald reportedly had been a member briefly, had been arrested in New Orleans shortly after the assassination, on a tip that he was involved with Oswald, and then released.[4] Carlos Quiroga, the exile who had visited Oswald's home several times in New Orleans, had done so for the purpose, he alleged, of appraising Oswald's pro-Castro activities.[5] W. Guy Banister was the private detective known to be associated with anti-Castro activists in New Orleans and had an office in a building whose address appeared on pro-Castro literature Oswald distributed.[6] All this information, it will be recalled, was in the hands of the Commission, yet none of these three men was questioned by the Commission or its staff. It seemed to me that leads such as these, if they had been pursued, could have provided a possible bridge between the known and unknown worlds of Lee Harvey Oswald in New Orleans. And once such a bridge was crossed, a whole new set of clues to why Oswald killed the President might have been found.

Could Garrison have discovered such a bridge? Skeptics tended to dismiss the possibility on the ground that Garrison was a flamboyant and extremely ambitious politician. According to Aaron M. Kohn, the managing director of the Metropolitan Crime Commission of New Orleans, "Garrison never lets the responsibilities of being a prosecutor interfere with being a politician." However, the fact that Garrison was politically motivated did not necessarily—to my mind, at least—preclude the possibility that he might be on to something. Whereas it might not always have been in the interests of the Warren Commission, which was concerned as much with dispelling doubts as with ascertaining facts, to pursue leads that might generate further doubts, or possibly damage the effectiveness of federal agencies,[7] an ambitious politician, it seemed to me, might well pursue leads to their conclusion, especially since solving "the case of the century," as Garrison called it, would certainly enhance his reputation. Convinced that it was possible—indeed, probable—that Garrison could find details of Oswald's affairs that the Commission had missed, I went to New Orleans shortly after Garrison announced that he was getting to the bottom of the "assassination plot" and had arrested Shaw.

Jim Garrison—he legally changed his given name from Earling Carothers to Jim when he first entered politics—claims to be both a "lone-wolf reformer," influenced by Ayn Rand's writings on individualism, and a Southern Populist in the tradition of Huey Long who, Garrison has said, "had all the political answers."[8] (One "political answer" Long found was the conspiracy issue. Louisiana's electorate tends to divide along both ethnic and geographic lines—between French-speaking Catholics in the South and Anglo-Saxon Protestants in the North; Orleaneans and the rural population; and Negroes and whites.[9] By charging that the Standard Oil Company and other "Eastern monopolies" were conspiring with the established politicians and "lying newspapers" to deprive the people of Louisiana of their fair share of the oil revenues produced in the state, Long raised an issue that cut across the traditional cleavages in the electorate, and tended to unite the "have-nots" against the "haves."[10] Whether the "oil conspiracy" was a real or fancied one is even today a hotly debated question in New Orleans.)

Ever since Garrison was first elected District Attorney, in 1961, he has been a controversial figure in New Orleans. He has fought long and hard against prostitutes, homosexuals in the French Quarter, and the more vulnerable purveyors of vice, but, according to his critics on the Metropolitan Crime Commission, he has neglected the problem of organized crime in New Orleans. "People worry about the crime 'syndicate,'" Garrison once said, "but the real danger is the political establishment, power massing against the individual."[11] When the city's eight criminal-court justices exercised their statutory right to oversee the financing of his anti-vice campaign, Garrison charged that their actions "raised interesting questions about racketeer influences." A court subsequently convicted Garrison of criminally libeling the eight judges, but the conviction was reversed by the U.S. Supreme Court, in a decision that held that individuals have the right to criticize public officials even though the charges may turn out to be unfounded.[12]

Garrison is popularly referred to in New Orleans as the Jolly Green Giant—an image conjured up by his imposing physical stature (six feet six inches) and his political glad hand. When I met him, in mid-April 1967, his welcome was gracious, if slightly fulsome; he told me, almost solemnly, that it was his reading of my book that first set him thinking about launching an investigation of his own. (Later, I learned that this was a standard greeting, extended to almost all critics of the Warren Commission.)

Dean Andrews had just been indicted on five counts of perjury, and Garrison seemed flushed with victory. "Personally I like Dean, everyone does," he said, "but I have to show him I mean business." Andrews, who it will be recalled is the lawyer who had told the Warren Commission that a mysterious figure named Clay Bertrand had phoned him after the assassination and suggested that he defend Oswald, had testified on his second appearance before the Orleans Parish Grand Jury that he could not identify Clay Bertrand as Clay Shaw.[13] Garrison said it was "obvious that Andrews was protecting Shaw." He was certain, at any rate, that Andrews would be convicted on at least one count of perjury: when he was an assistant district attorney in neighboring Jefferson Parish, Andrews had, in his private practice, helped a client (a friend of Ferrie's) obtain a parole—illegal under Louisiana law. "We purposely asked Andrews about that in front of the grand jury," Garrison explained, and Andrews denied it (otherwise, he would have had to incriminate himself).

Over a leisurely dinner at Broussard's, Garrison began to tell me about the conspiracy he had uncovered. It was a diffuse narrative, in which it appeared, as noted earlier, that Oswald had only been feigning the role he went to considerable lengths to establish for himself as a pro-Castroite; Garrison said Oswald had in fact been part of an *anti*-Castro assassination team trained by David Ferrie. Ferrie, in turn, was in some important way—Garrison never explained exactly how—personally involved with Clay Shaw. When a plan to shoot Castro was aborted because Oswald could not obtain a visa to Cuba, the assassination team turned its attention to President Kennedy, and, on November 22, 1963, carried out its mission.

How had Garrison discovered this conspiracy? "It's exactly like a chess problem," he explained. "The Warren Commission moved the same pieces back and forth and got nowhere. I made a new move and solved the problem." The move he meant was the arrest of Clay Shaw. He pointed out that after Shaw was arrested, men from the District Attorney's office searched Shaw's home, in the French Quarter, and found in it a cache of new evidence, which he suggested that I should see, because it would give me "a new perspective on the case."

Early the next morning, I went to the District Attorney's office, which is housed, next to the Parish Prison, in the Criminal District Court Building, a massive structure at Tulane Avenue and South Broad. Garrison had not yet arrived, but one of his assistants, James C. Alcock, told me that Garrison had left word that I should "start going through the evidence." I did so with Jones Harris, a New Yorker of independent means who had devoted the better part of the last three years to a private investigation of the assassination. Six cardboard cartons were brought out containing personal belongings of Clay Shaw: letters, photographs, financial records, blueprints for renovating houses in the French Quarter, the manuscripts of plays he had written years ago, calendars, checkbooks, address books. In one box were a black costume, a net mask, and some plastic slippers—all of which Shaw had claimed were part of his 1965 Mardi Gras costume.[14] Alcock said that the District Attorney's staff had yet to examine all this material, and he suggested that Harris and I look through Shaw's address books and financial records in hopes of discovering some information that might interest Garrison. We were left alone with the evidence.

Though none of these materials, as far as I could see after examining them, had anything directly to do with the assassination, the odd way in which Garrison treated them did give me, when I thought about it later, "a new perspective on the case." I recalled that a judge's order had forbidden discussion or disclosure of any evidence in the case.[15] The very fact that Harris and I were allowed to examine objects seized from Shaw's home and designated "evidence" seemed to be a direct violation of that order. Why, I wondered, should the District Attorney risk having his case thrown out of court on a technicality by letting outsiders go freely through the evidence? Moreover, it seemed curious that Clay Shaw's papers had not already been rigorously scrutinized by Garrison or his staff, especially since Garrison had told several people, including me, that one of the main reasons for arresting Clay Shaw on March 1 was to prevent him from destroying his personal papers. Six weeks had passed, and yet from what I saw it appeared that no real investigation of Clay Shaw was going on at all—but only a search for peripheral characters connected with David Ferrie. If Garrison believed that Shaw had openly conspired to kill the President, why was the inquiry into his activities being treated with such apparent nonchalance?

A discovery that Jones Harris made while we were going through the papers provided considerable insight into the nature of Garrison's investigation. What Harris found was a five-digit number that was common to both Shaw's and Oswald's address books. The entry in Shaw's book was "Lee Odom, PO Box 19106, Dallas, Tex." In Oswald's book, the number 19106 was preceded by the Cyrillic letters      (which, like other Russian letters on the page, the Warren Commission had assumed were made during Oswald's two-and-a-half-year stay in the Soviet Union). Though the coincidence of numbers proved nothing in itself, it was striking, and Garrison decided that further investigation was merited. Shortly thereafter, Garrison announced to the press that he had found the entry "PO

19106" in both Oswald's and Shaw's address books, and that the number was a "nonexistent or fictional number," which removed "the possibility of coincidence." Moreover, Garrison said that "PO 19106" was a code that, when deciphered, produced Jack Ruby's unlisted telephone number, WH 1-5601, and "no other number on earth."[16] The method by which Garrison "deciphered" the code is worth following. Starting with the "scrambled" number 19106, Garrison "unscrambled" it (by choosing the nearest digit, then the farthest, then the next nearest, etc.) to produce the number 16901. Ruby's number was 15601, so by unscrambling the digits Garrison managed to match the last two digits in the two numbers. The next step was to subtract the arbitrary number 1300 from 16901, and—presto—15601.[17] Finally, Garrison converted the prefix "PO" to "WH" by a system that, according to the prominent cryptographer Irwin Mann, yields at least six different prefixes; Garrison chose Ruby's.[18]

A few days after Garrison announced that he had deciphered the code, it became known that the number 19106 in Shaw's address book was by no means "nonexistent or fictional." PO Box 19106 had been, as Shaw's address book indicated, the address in Dallas of a man named Lee Odom. Odom stated that he had been introduced to Shaw in 1966 by the manager of the Roosevelt Hotel in New Orleans, and had briefly discussed with Shaw the possibility of bringing bloodless bullfights to New Orleans; he had left his business address—PO Box 19106, Dallas, Texas—with Shaw.[19] In fact, Odom's post-office box could not possibly have been the number in Oswald's book, because the post-

office-box number 19106 did not exist in Dallas before
it was assigned to Odom, in 1965—long after Oswald's
death, in 1963. It was clear that Garrison had done
some questionable interpolating of his own in mov-
ing from a coincidence to a conspiracy. First, he had
told newsmen that the number in Oswald's book was
PO 19106, although in fact it was      19106. (When a
television interviewer later asked him how he had
determined that the prefix was PO, rather than      , he
answered, with perfect aplomb, "More or less by looking at it.")[20] Then, without first checking with the Dallas post office whether in fact such an address existed,
he had announced that the post-office-box number was
fictional. And, finally, he had converted the number
in Shaw's book into Jack Ruby's phone number by
rearranging the digits, subtracting an arbitrary number, and changing the letters "PO" to "WH." Garrison
had constructed a piece of evidence against Clay
Shaw and had disclosed it to the press. Yet the District
Attorney did not seem particularly perturbed when
questions were raised about the logic of his deduc-
tions. When he was asked on a local television show
how the number of a post-office box that didn't exist
until 1965 could have been used to represent Jack
Ruby's phone number in 1963, he replied, "Well, that's
a problem for you to think over, because you obviously
missed the point."[21] Indeed, Garrison counterattacked
in a press conference, saying, "We are very interested
in knowing who introduced Mr. Odom to Mr. Shaw,
how many bullfights Mr. Odom has actually produced"
—as if this fact were relevant to his investigation—and,
"We are particularly interested in clarifying now why

there is also coded in Lee Oswald's address book the local phone number of the Central Intelligence Agency." Using an entirely different system of decipherment—multiplying the number by 10, rearranging the digits, subtracting 1700, and remultiplying— Garrison managed to convert the number 1147, which appeared in Oswald's book, to 522-8874, the CIA's phone number. Oswald's codes were "subjective," Garrison said, in that they varied from number to number.[22] There seemed little point in Oswald's having gone through such an elaborate procedure, however, because the CIA number that Garrison referred to was— and is—listed in the New Orleans telephone book.*

What was Garrison's purpose in all this flimflammery? He himself noted, in an extended interview in *Playboy* for October 1967, that pre-trial publicity prejudicial to the defendant "could get our whole case thrown out of court," yet he himself had jeopardized his case by releasing information that was not only prejudicial to Clay Shaw but unfounded. The story about PO Box 19106 evidently was not part of his pending court case; otherwise presumably he would have kept it secret from the defense and carefully investigated it. It did, however, raise some questions about Garrison's investigation.

---

* Garrison subsequently used another telephone number in an attempt to link Oswald and Ruby: "If you look in Oswald's address book, you will see PE 8–1951. . . . Jack Ruby called that number twice. It is a number in Fort Worth. . . . There was indeed a close relation between Lee Oswald and Jack Ruby."[23] What Garrison omitted to say was that PE 8–1951 was—and is—the telephone number of a television station in Fort Worth.

# ▐▐

# The Suspect

There will be arrests, charges and convictions.
This is no Mickey Mouse investigation.

—Jim Garrison, February 25, 1967,
Associated Press

It was aboard a jet flight between New Orleans and New York in late November of 1966 that the Garrison investigation started taking shape. Prompted by stories in the national media that called for a new investigation into the assassination, three prominent passengers —Senator Russell B. Long, of Louisiana; Joseph M. Rault, Jr., a wealthy New Orleans oilman; and District Attorney Jim Garrison—began speculating about the events in Dallas three years before. As their conversation was reported in *New Orleans*, the official magazine of the city's Chamber of Commerce, the three agreed that, in Rault's words, ". . . it would be almost preposterous to believe that one man, an individual such as Oswald, could have been the only one involved in

33

this thing." Senator Long cited deficiencies in the Warren Commission's investigation. "I think if I were investigating," he said, "I'd find the hundred best riflemen in the world and find the ones who were in Dallas that day." Garrison recalled that in 1963 his office had been interested in "a very unusual type of person who made a very curious trip at a very curious time about the date of the assassination," and the District Attorney added that he "might want to now go back into some of those events."[1]

The individual whom Garrison had in mind was David Ferrie, and he was, to say the least of it, "a very unusual type of person." Garrison later characterized Ferrie as both an "evil genius" and "a pathetic and tortured creature."[2] To compensate for being completely hairless, Ferrie pasted what looked like clumps of red monkey fur on his head and wore artificial eyebrows. Explanations of how Ferrie lost his hair have become part of the folklore of the assassination. William W. Turner, author of a so-called official history of the Garrison investigation which appeared in *Ramparts* (and a former employee of the FBI), reported one speculation that the loss might have been "a physiological reaction to exposure to the extreme altitudes required for clandestine flights." He went on to say that Chinese Nationalist U-2 pilots have reportedly experienced the same "hair-loss phenomenon."[3] Fred Powledge, after interviewing Garrison, wrote in the *New Republic* that Ferrie's "interest in homosexuality led him to shave off all his body hair."[4] However, the question was decisively answered by Harold Weisberg, a critic of the Warren Commission, whose stepbrother,

Dr. Jack Kety, had treated Ferrie for the disease alopecia, which can render its victims hairless.[5]

Rather like Oswald, Ferrie was a failure at virtually everything he tried. He trained for the priesthood, and was dismissed from two seminaries as a result of eccentric personal behavior. Later, he became a "bishop" in a quasi-political underground cult called the Orthodox Old Catholic Church of North America. For a while, Ferrie ran a service station in New Orleans. His greatest ambition, however, seems to have been to become a fighter pilot. In 1950, he wrote to Secretary of Defense Louis A. Johnson, demanding, "When am I going to get the commission, when the Russians are bombing the hell out of Cleveland?" In a letter to the commanding officer of the First Air Force, he wrote, "There is nothing I would enjoy better than blowing the hell out of every damn Russian, Communist, Red or what-have-you. . . . Between my friends and I we can cook up a crew that can really blow them to hell. . . . I want to train killers, however bad that sounds. It is what we need."[6] Ferrie never received an Air Force commission, but he did succeed in becoming the leader of a unit in the Civil Air Patrol (a civilian organization made up of volunteers), and he also set himself to training youths in jungle-warfare tactics.[7] Oswald, according to a witness before the Warren Commission named Edward Voebel, belonged to Ferrie's outfit for a brief time in the nineteen-fifties —and even may have attended a Civil Air Patrol party at Ferrie's home, when he was a teen-ager.[8] Ferrie was also engaged in a long-term project to discover a cure for cancer, and it was said that at one time he housed thousands of white mice in his apartment in New Orleans.[9] For a while, he was employed as a pilot for Eastern Airlines, but he was suspended, in 1961, as a consequence of an arrest on a morals charge, and later dismissed. After that, he managed to make a meager living as a free-lance pilot, an independent psychologist, a hypnotist, and a private detective.[10]

Ferrie also became quite interested in Cuban affairs. In the mid-nineteen-fifties, while Fidel Castro was waging a guerrilla war against the Batista regime in Cuba, Ferrie attempted to raise funds for Castro. Captain Neville Levy, a New Orleans businessman, recalled that Ferrie carried a loaded army revolver with him while soliciting contributions for Castro's campaign.[11] After Castro came to power, Ferrie became rabidly anti-Castro. He approached Sergio Arcacha Smith, the leader of the Cuban Democratic Revolutionary Front in New Orleans—an anti-Castro coalition—and volunteered to train recruits for an invasion of Cuba.[12] He also, according to Diego Gonzales Tendedera, the Miami correspondent for *El Tiempo*, flew firebomb raids against Cuba and helped anti-Castro refugees escape until 1961, when federal agents confiscated the plane he was using.[13] After the Bay of Pigs invasion in April 1961, Ferrie said in a speech to the New Orleans chapter of the Military Orders of World Wars that he had been a pilot in the abortive invasion, and then went on to criticize President Kennedy for failing to provide the necessary air support for the anti-Castro forces.[14] In 1962, perhaps finally realizing his desire to "train killers," he reportedly drilled anti-Castroites in paramilitary tactics in St. Tammany Parish, across Lake Pontchartrain from New Orleans.[15]

In 1963, Ferrie was employed as a private investigator for the law firm then representing Carlos Marcello, who was reputed to be the head of the New Orleans Mafia. Marcello had been deported in an extralegal manner—he was abducted by Justice Department agents and put on a plane to Guatemala. According to one story, Ferrie clandestinely flew Marcello back into this country.[16] On the day of the assassination, Ferrie claimed, he was in court, listening to a judge declare the Marcello deportation illegal. To celebrate the victory, Ferrie drove to Texas on a "goose-hunting" expedition with two friends. Meanwhile, Garrison's office received the tip from New Orleans private detective Jack Martin (who had worked for W. Guy Banister) to the effect that Ferrie had trained Oswald in marksmanship and was Oswald's "getaway pilot." Martin was said to be a member of the same cult in which Ferrie was a bishop. On his return to New Orleans, Ferrie was arrested and questioned, but, according to FBI reports, Martin admitted that he had made up the whole story, and Ferrie was released.[17]

The FBI may not have thought much of Martin's tip, but it was this tip that enabled Garrison to begin his investigation, in December 1966, with a specific suspect in mind—David Ferrie. Garrison set about his work with the assistance of a small but industrious staff. His chief investigator, a policeman named Louis Ivon, had requisitioned other members of the New

Orleans Police Department to do the necessary leg-
work. William H. Gurvich, a partner in one of the
city's largest private-detective agencies, served as one
of Garrison's chief aides for six months, handling in-
terrogations and the extraterritorial aspects of the investigation. Thomas Bethell, a young British writer
who was living in New Orleans, was put in charge
of research. Assistant District Attorneys Alcock, Andrew J. Sciambra, Richard V. Burnes, and Alvin V.
Oser questioned the more important witnesses and prepared the legal groundwork. Other tasks were performed by some of Garrison's personal friends—among
them Max Gonzales, a law clerk in the criminal court
and a pilot, who made a number of flights with Ferrie
in order to gain his confidence, and Alberto Fowler,
a Cuban exile and the Director of International Relations for the City of New Orleans, who made discreet
inquiries about Ferrie's activities among anti-Castro
exiles. Later, a self-styled intelligence expert using the
pseudonym Bill Boxley joined Garrison's staff.* Although during its early stages the investigation was
generally kept secret from the press, two members of
*Life* magazine's staff, David L. Chandler, the New
Orleans reporter, and Richard N. Billings, an associate
editor, participated in what Garrison described as "an
information exchange" and were permitted to observe
the interrogation of witnesses, polygraph (or lie-detector) tests, and staff meetings.

Garrison began his investigation in December 1966
by compiling a dossier on Ferrie. Cameras were secretly

---

* Garrison subsequently identified "Boxley" as William C. Wood, and
claimed that he was a former CIA employee.

set up across from Ferrie's apartment, he was followed everywhere he went, and his friends were questioned about his activities. Garrison even attempted to plant an "undercover agent" in Ferrie's private coterie. Little came of this surveillance.[18] For further information, Garrison turned back to Martin, whose tip had first linked Oswald and Ferrie. Martin, who told Secret Service agents that he suffers from "telephonitis" when he has taken a drink and that it was on such an occasion that he telephoned the District Attorney's office about Ferrie,[19] continued to narrate a vast number of disconnected yarns about Ferrie and the assassination. According to a typical one of these, Ferrie hypnotized Oswald and then dispatched him on the assassination mission. According to another, Ferrie had a working association with certain anti-Castro activities conducted by the private detective W. Guy Banister. Garrison found this connection especially provocative, because of the offices that Banister, up to the time of his death, in 1964, maintained in a building one of whose addresses was 544 Camp Street, a block from the William B. Reily Company, where Oswald worked. One of the questions the Warren Commission had left unanswered was why the "544 Camp Street" address appeared as Oswald's headquarters on some pro-Castro literature that he possessed. Since Banister's office was, as Garrison put it, "a mare's-nest of anti-Castro activity," Garrison postulated that Oswald might be an "agent provocateur" in Banister's employ.[20]

Garrison followed up this lead by systematically questioning Banister's former employees. One of them, a shipping clerk and sometime private investigator named David F. Lewis, Jr., added richly to the developing drama. Lewis claimed that he had been witness to a meeting among Banister, Ferrie, the anti-Castro leader Carlos Quiroga, and a person he called Leon Oswald, who he later thought might be Lee Harvey Oswald. Although Lewis said he was certain that this meeting had occurred in 1962, a time when Oswald was known to be living in Texas,[21] and although Quiroga categorically denied that such a meeting had ever taken place, Garrison intensified his efforts in this direction. He began digging into the activities of anti-Castro Cubans, and discovered the sites of what had been two secret training camps in St. Tammany Parish.[22] (One of them was rumored to have been the site of the Ferrie anti-Castro drills and commando training.) In the hope of identifying the men under Ferrie's command, Garrison hired Bernardo Torres, a private detective from Miami who claimed to have assisted the Secret Service by spotting potentially dangerous Cubans during a visit President Kennedy made to Miami in 1963. In December 1966 and January 1967 the investigation was broadened to include various efforts to track down, with Torres' help, any Cubans in Miami who might have known Ferrie. These efforts turned out to be unproductive but quite expensive—more than half the total expenditures up to that time—and Garrison began to suspect that Torres' activity did not justify the expense. Toward the end of January, the Florida manhunt was called off.[23]

But Garrison had other leads to follow—notably the old clue from New Orleans lawyer Dean Andrews. Andrews' original story, it will be recalled, which he told to the Secret Service shortly after the assassination, was that Oswald had come to his office a few times during the summer of 1963 in the hope of finding some means by which the "undesirable" discharge he had been given by the Marine Corps could be converted into an honorable one. The day after the assassination, Andrews, who was in the hospital under sedation recovering from pneumonia, said he received a phone call from a man he knew as Clay Bertrand, whom he described as "a lawyer without a briefcase" for local homosexuals. According to Andrews, Bertrand asked him to go to Dallas and defend Oswald. When Andrews was questioned by the FBI, he gave several different descriptions of Bertrand, and finally said that the character bearing that name was merely a figment of his imagination. A few months later, he again changed his story, telling the Warren Commission that he had recently seen Bertrand in a bar, and describing him as "a boy" who was "five foot eight inches" and had "sandy hair." He explained that he had finally told the FBI agents who interviewed him, "Write what you want, that I am nuts"—because, as he put it, "They are on you like the plague. They never leave. They are like cancer. Eternal."[24] No other clues to Bertrand's identity turned up, however, and Wesley J. Liebeler, the Commission lawyer who conducted the investigation in this area, said he was convinced that no such person existed.*

---

* When I interviewed Andrews in June 1967, he told me that he had made up the name " 'Clay Bertrand' out of solid air" to protect a friend. He explained that on the night after the assassination he received a phone call from the friend, who vaguely knew Oswald as an infrequent customer in a "gay bar" that he owned in the French

Garrison nevertheless now decided to pursue the matter further, and gave Assistant District Attorney Sciambra, a former boxer known by the nickname Moo, a task he referred to as "squeezing" the French Quarter. A crackdown on homosexuals that Garrison had carried out in 1962 was generally thought to have produced a number of informers, but Sciambra was unable to find anyone who had ever heard of Clay Bertrand.[25] Garrison reasoned that Dean Andrews was probably protecting a wealthy client with homosexual associates, and came up with the idea that Clay Bertrand was in reality Clay Shaw, the socially prominent retired director of the International Trade Mart in New Orleans.[26] David Chandler, the *Life* reporter who worked closely with Garrison in the early days of the investigation, was present when Garrison first put forward this hypothesis to his staff. According to Chandler, Garrison offered three arguments for it. First, Shaw had the same first name as Bertrand. Second, Shaw was rumored to have friends in the homosexual world. And, finally, Shaw spoke fluent Spanish and, although Andrews had never said that Bertrand spoke Spanish, Garrison was looking for a conspirator involved in anti-Castro activities.[27] Garrison brushed over the fact that Shaw—six feet four and a quarter inches tall, fifty-four years old,

---

Quarter. It was this friend, Andrews said, who had recommended him to Oswald as an attorney who might help him "fix" his "undesirable" discharge from the Marine Corps, and now he thought Andrews "could pick up some publicity" by appearing in Dallas as Oswald's lawyer. When the FBI became interested, Andrews explained, he invented the name "Clay Bertrand" to divert their attention from the real person who had phoned him. When I asked why he had told a Warren Commission lawyer that he had recently seen Clay Bertrand, he replied, "Aw, I was just putting the guy on a little."

and white-haired—hardly fitted Andrews' description of a five-foot-eight-inch boy with sandy hair. He also ignored the question of why Andrews, having given a false description and a false last name to protect his client, would give the client's correct first name.

In any event, Shaw was brought in for questioning in late December, on the pretext that Garrison was attempting to tie up a few loose ends in the Warren Report. According to Chandler, it quickly became apparent that Shaw had no information to offer about Ferrie or his activities, and the matter was dropped. The District Attorney told his staff to "forget Shaw." In January, when asked if he knew the identity of Clay Bertrand by Richard Billings of *Life*, who spent a good deal of time with Garrison during this period, Garrison replied, "His real name is Clay Shaw, but I don't think he's too important." Ferrie was still, at this time, the only suspect.[28]

By February 1967, the investigation seemed to be at a standstill. Ferrie obviously knew that he was under suspicion, and it was highly unlikely that he would do anything to incriminate himself. The Cuban-exile trail had petered out in Miami. The Bertrand matter had been shelved. Garrison's chief witness was still David Lewis, and, of the four participants in the meeting that Lewis described, Oswald and Banister were dead, Quiroga (according to Garrison) could not be found,* and Ferrie unequivocally denied everything.

---

* Quiroga claims that he was in New Orleans during this entire period, except for a two-week vacation, and that he was questioned on January 21, 1967, by Garrison's representatives. He completely denied the Lewis story, and apparently the District Attorney preferred to designate him a missing witness.

At this point, Gordon Novel, a specialist in anti-eavesdropping devices, was recommended to Garrison by Willard E. Robertson, a New Orleans automobile dealer who was one of Garrison's political supporters. (Garrison had been so concerned that the FBI might be tapping his telephones that he had made plans a few weeks before to execute a midnight raid on the FBI field office in New Orleans, using a water pistol loaded with a charge of red pepper to disarm the officer on duty; he even invited Chandler, the *Life* reporter, to accompany him on the mission, but for some reason the plan was scrapped.)[29] Upon learning that Ferrie was under suspicion, Novel told Garrison that he knew a good deal about Ferrie's activities in 1961. According to Garrison, Novel claimed that Ferrie, Cuban-exile leader Sergio Arcacha Smith, and two unidentified Cubans had been involved in a "pickup" of arms from a bunker in Houma, Louisiana, belonging to the Schlumberger Well Surveying Corporation. Some of the arms were reportedly deposited in the offices of W. Guy Banister. The purpose of the raid was to acquire arms for an anti-Castro militia, and Novel stated that a CIA contact had indulgently provided a key to the bunker.[30] Novel later claimed that one of Garrison's ideas for breaking the stalemate his investigation had apparently reached involved a plot to kidnap Ferrie. According to this story, Ferrie was to be shot with an atropine dart, injected with sodium pentothal, and forced to confess.[31] Novel has said, "Garrison asked me to order him such a dart gun so that it wouldn't appear on his office purchase records" after the District Attorney "had read about the idea in one of the books about the CIA."[32]

The entire investigation might have expired quietly for want of any truly tangible leads if it had not been for some resourceful moves by three reporters for the New Orleans *States-Item*—Rosemary James, Jack Dempsey, and David Snyder. In New Orleans, the financial vouchers of the District Attorney's office are a matter of public record. By piecing together information gleaned from these records and through various leaks from Garrison's office, the reporters were able to come up with a fairly accurate picture of the investigation, even though it was still being kept secret. Mrs. James wrote an article on the subject and showed it to Garrison on February 16, 1967. He simply shrugged and told her, "I will neither confirm nor deny it."[33] The next day, the story broke. Garrison's investigation into the assassination of President Kennedy was now a public issue. Garrison charged that the news story had seriously interfered with his efforts; arrests that were to have been made immediately, he claimed, had now to be deferred for months. Moreover, he announced that he would seek private financing in order not to have to conduct the inquiry in a "fishbowl." Two political allies, Joseph Rault (who had been on the fateful plane trip with Garrison and Senator Long) and Willard Robertson, thereupon organized fifty New Orleans businessmen into a group that called itself Truth or Consequences, Inc.[34] Its function was to supply Garrison with both funds and moral support. Meanwhile, David Ferrie told a newspaperman that Garrison's investigation, in which he was suspected of being Oswald's getaway pilot, was nothing but "a big joke." He denied that he knew Oswald, and, for good measure, added that he was conducting his own inquiry into the assassination.

For two days, shortly after the *States-Item* broke the news of Garrison's investigation, Ferrie was kept under "protective custody," Billings has reported, at the Fontainebleau Motor Hotel in New Orleans.[35] According to a member of Garrison's staff, this was done at Ferrie's request. In any event, he returned to his own apartment on the evening of February 21. The next day, Ferrie was found dead. An autopsy indicated that he had died of a cerebral hemorrhage caused by the rupture of a blood vessel. The coroner, Dr. Nicholas Chetta, ruled out suicide, because a person is rarely aware that an aneurysm, or weak spot, exists in a blood vessel, and it would be virtually impossible to induce a "blowout." He also ruled out murder, on the ground that if the rupture had been caused by an external blow there would necessarily have been tissue damage, and none was found. He concluded that Ferrie had died from natural causes.[36] But the mere fact that a man suspected of having conspired to assassinate the President had died five days after he was publicly implicated in the crime was sensational news, and reporters flocked to New Orleans. Garrison interpreted a somewhat ambiguous letter that Ferrie wrote to a friend shortly before his death as a "suicide note," and, without waiting for the results of the autopsy, proclaimed Ferrie's death a suicide. Garrison called Ferrie

"one of history's most important individuals," and
claimed that an arrest had been only days away. "Apparently, we waited too long," he said.[37] No mention
was made of the fact that Ferrie had already been
placed effectively under protective custody for two
days.

Ferrie's death brought a windfall of publicity, but
Garrison had lost his prime suspect. And the hundreds
of newsmen who had come to New Orleans could
hardly be expected to continue reporting cryptic comments from Garrison such as "The key to the whole
case is through the looking glass. Black is white; white
is black." When they asked for hard news, Garrison
told them that he had "positively solved the assassination of President John F. Kennedy," and he added
that arrests might take as long as "thirty years."[38]
At that point, most of the out-of-town reporters left.
Headlines are made of arrests and deaths, not long-
term promises.

Garrison, though, had promised that arrests would
be forthcoming, and a number of possible suspects
were hastily considered. Some were drawn from Ferrie's twilight world of adventurers and self-styled
secret agents.[39] Others, according to William Gurvich,
were prominent citizens of New Orleans—the president
of a food-processing company, a hotel magnate, a
nationally known physician.[40] At this point, Garrison
received a brief letter from Perry Raymond Russo, a
twenty-five-year-old Baton Rouge insurance salesman,
who claimed to have information about Ferrie "that
might or might not be valuable."[41] This very much

interested Garrison, and in the next seven days Russo's story became quite "valuable" to the District Attorney.

### The Development of Russo's Story: A Chronology

*February 24*: While Russo was waiting for a reply from Garrison, he approached a number of local reporters with his story, and taped a television interview with James Kemp of WDSU-TV in New Orleans. Asked whether Ferrie had made any threatening remarks about President Kennedy, Russo said, "[Ferrie] talked in general terms, not specifically about Kennedy, about how easy it would be to assassinate a President of the United States because of the fact he was in public view so much and unprotected more or less, and there were so many people and the availability of exit and the fact that he could drive a plane to get out of the country, and he used to posingly, jokingly pose the question that, you know, he and I could do it; you know, just in a joking way, he said it could be done. And that was all of the conversation during the summer." Russo also stated flatly in the interview, "I never heard of Oswald until the television of the assassination."[42]

*February 25*: The day after Garrison received Russo's letter, Moo Sciambra was sent to Baton Rouge to question Russo. The greater part of the interview was confined to uncovering Russo's relationship with Ferrie. Russo told Sciambra that he had first met Ferrie in 1962, when he attempted to get a young friend of his in Ferrie's Civil Air Patrol unit out from under what he called the commander's "spell." Russo said that at one point, after he had succeeded in breaking Ferrie's hold over his friend, Ferrie had threatened to kill him. Later, however, he and Ferrie became friends, and worked as partners in selling pornographic films imported from Cuba. Ferrie's main interests, Russo continued, were, first, instructing members of his Civil Air Patrol outfit in "the art of fighting jungle warfare" and, second, his medical research; he was developing an aphrodisiac for homosexuals as well as a cure for cancer. But Ferrie had said very little to him on the subject of assassination, except for some vague remarks about how easy it would be to shoot a President and flee by airplane to Cuba or Brazil. Russo indicated that Ferrie probably had in mind either Eisenhower or the President of Mexico. He did remember, however, that Ferrie had said a few times in the summer of 1963 that he would "get" Kennedy. Sciambra then showed Russo some photographs. The first one he identified was of Sergio Arcacha Smith, the Cuban-exile leader. Russo identified him as an actor in one of the pornographic films. "To be perfectly honest," he said, "I looked at the film quite a bit." (Russo was mistaken in his identification. Garrison's investigators later ascertained that the actor in the film was not Arcacha Smith.) The second photograph was of Clay Shaw. Russo said that he thought he had seen this man from a distance twice before but that he never met him. The last photograph showed Lee Harvey Oswald. Russo thought this person might have been a roommate of Ferrie's, who had a beard.[43]

*February 26:* The next day, back in New Orleans, Sciambra gave Garrison a preliminary oral report on his interview with Russo in the presence of Richard Billings, of *Life*. Garrison then asked Sciambra to arrange a test for Russo using "truth serum," or sodium pentothal.[44]

*February 27*: The next morning Russo came to Garrison's office, and Sciambra drafted a long memorandum to Garrison concerning his interview on February 25 with Russo in Baton Rouge. Later, sodium pentothal was administered to Russo by the coroner, Dr. Chetta, at Mercy Hospital. While under the influence of the drug, Russo was again questioned by Sciambra, though no transcript was made of the interrogation. But afterward, Sciambra prepared a memorandum on the results of the sodium-pentothal session which states that Russo made a passing reference to a party in Ferrie's apartment during which a plot was discussed—but only after Sciambra had prompted him by asking "if he could remember any of the details about Clay Bertrand being up in Ferrie's apartment." The name Bertrand was first mentioned, the memorandum indicates, by Moo Sciambra. Later that evening, Russo had dinner with Garrison, Sciambra, and Billings, and Sciambra told Russo that after taking truth serum he had identified a tall man with white kinky hair, and that he had also said that he had been introduced to this man as "Bertrand" at Ferrie's apartment. According to Billings, Russo insisted that he did not remember ever having met anyone named Bertrand. Garrison attempted to resolve this embarrassing discrepancy by suggesting to Billings that the truth serum probably jogged Russo's memory.[45] "They asked me a lot of questions," Russo is reported to have recalled later. "I could figure out what they wanted to know."[46]

*February 28*: The following day, Garrison brought Russo to Shaw's home in the French Quarter for a look at Shaw. Russo rang Shaw's doorbell and introduced himself as a Mutual of Omaha insurance salesman, then returned to the car where Sciambra was waiting for him and, according to Sciambra, identified Clay Shaw as the man he had been introduced to as Bertrand in Ferrie's apartment.[47]

*March 1*: Garrison summoned Shaw to his office and had him interrogated for two and a half hours. Shaw categorically denied that he knew either Ferrie or Oswald and that he knew anything about the assassination. When the topic of using truth serum came up, Shaw sent for a lawyer, Salvatore Panzeca. Panzeca agreed to let Shaw take a lie-detector test, provided that the defense had the right to approve the wording of the questions, that the results of the test were not disclosed except at a duly authorized court proceeding, and that Shaw had a day's rest before the test. Garrison replied that he did not have to agree to any conditions. A moment later, he declared that Shaw was under arrest, had him handcuffed, and led him before news photographers to be booked.[48] Then he applied for a warrant from Criminal Court Judge Matthew S. Braniff to search Clay Shaw's premises, stating in his application that a "confidential informer" had told of a meeting in which "David W. Ferrie, Lee Harvey Oswald, and Clay Shaw (alias Clay Bertrand) were discussing how they would kill John F. Kennedy." The arrest, Garrison later told me, was "a command decision." He said he was apprehensive that if he released Shaw the suspect might "destroy vital evidence." This explanation made little sense, for Garrison could have obtained a search warrant without arresting Shaw, no more cause was required than that he have a confidential informant, and he had—Perry Russo. Moreover, he had questioned Shaw in December, and if Shaw had had incriminating evidence in his home it would seem likely that he would have disposed of it then. But, whatever Garrison's motives were, on March 1, 1967, a week after the death of Ferrie, Clay Shaw was arrested for conspiring to murder John F. Kennedy.

# The Witnesses

I've taken unusual steps to protect the right of the
defendant and assure him a fair trial. Before we
introduced the testimony of our witnesses, we
made them undergo independent verifying tests,
including polygraph examination, truth serum, and
hypnosis. We thought this would be hailed as an
unprecedented step in jurisprudence. . . .

—Jim Garrison, October 1967, *Playboy*

In Louisiana, after an arrest has been made, the district attorney either presents the case to a grand jury
or files a "bill of information," which, under the Louisiana code of criminal procedure, allows a district attorney to bring a case to trial without a grand-jury indictment. In the case of Clay Shaw, however, Garrison
decided to do something that was, in his own words,
"virtually unheard of."[1] Instead of going before a
grand jury meeting in closed session, he requested
a preliminary hearing, which takes place before a
judge and is public. The purpose of a preliminary
hearing under Louisiana law is to determine whether
or not the state has sufficient evidence to warrant a
trial. Although it is not unusual for the defense to

request a preliminary hearing, if only to attempt to compel the state to tip its hand and disclose vital evidence before the actual trial, such a hearing is rarely, if ever, requested by the prosecution. Why, then, should Garrison, the prosecutor, have elected to disclose some of his evidence before the trial—an apparently gratuitous favor to the defense? Garrison has said that he did so in order to "lean over backward and give the defendant every chance."[2] A preliminary hearing, however, has at least one extralegal consequence that a political-minded prosecutor might find advantageous: it provides the prosecution with a dramatic opportunity to reveal publicly far in advance of the trial some of the more sensational aspects of the case, thus helping to stimulate public interest. Whether or not Garrison's extraordinary move did, as he claimed, enhance the defendant's prospects for justice, it unquestionably worked to focus national attention on the case.

With a full complement of reporters in attendance, the hearing began on March 14, before a panel of three judges, with the testimony of Perry Russo, who was Garrison's surprise witness. Russo testified that he had known David Ferrie since 1960 and had an "open-book invitation" to visit Ferrie's apartment whenever he wanted to. On one such visit in September 1963, Russo said, he had encountered a young bearded man with an "old-fashion bolt-action rifle," to whom Ferrie subsequently introduced him as his roommate, "Leon Oswald." A few days later, Russo attended a party at Ferrie's apartment which eventually, Russo continued, "narrowed down to three persons besides myself"—

David Ferrie, "Leon Oswald" (whom Russo identified from a photograph as Lee Harvey Oswald), and a man he called Clem Bertrand. Then Garrison asked Russo whether he recognized "Clem Bertrand" in the courtroom. Russo pointed out Clay Shaw; then, at Garrison's request, walked over to Shaw and held his hand over his head.[3]

The witness then went on to testify that the three men planned the assassination of President Kennedy in his presence. "Ferrie took the initiative in the talk, pacing back and forth," Russo said. "He was talking to both Mr. Bertrand and Mr. Oswald, discussing diversionary tactics." He testified that after the three men had talked about such details as the "triangulation of cross fire," the selection of an appropriate "scapegoat," and the "availability of exits," they ended the conversation by bickering over various methods of escape.[4]

## Cross-Examination

Under cross-examination the following day, Russo admitted that he had not been able to identify Oswald positively until after an artist in the District Attorney's office had spent six hours drawing different beards on photographs of Oswald.[5] Russo's television statement of February 24—that he had "never heard of Oswald until the television of the assassination"—was also brought out. Asked by F. Irvin Dymond, Shaw's defense counsel, why he had denied, a few days before Garrison interrogated him, having known Oswald, Russo replied: "I knew Leon Oswald, who was slightly whiskered. . . . I did not, myself, honestly, know a Lee Harvey Oswald." Pressing Russo on the apparent contradiction between the statement he made in the television interview and his courtroom testimony, Dymond asked, "Are you testifying now that you knew Oswald, Leon Oswald, here in New Orleans, that you have identified a picture of Lee Harvey Oswald as the same man, and that after seeing the picture of Lee Harvey Oswald, roughly one hundred times, you still did not know it was the same, that it was the man you knew here in New Orleans?" Russo explained that the picture he had in his mind of Lee Harvey Oswald "was not identical" with that of the "Leon Oswald" he knew in New Orleans.[6]

Dymond also questioned the plausibility of Russo's story, asking him to explain why the alleged conspirators allowed him to overhear their plans to assassinate President Kennedy. Russo replied that Oswald and Bertrand were uneasy about his presence at the meeting until Ferrie said, "Forget him, he is all right, he don't know anything, and it don't make any difference with him." No one, Russo said, even cautioned him not to discuss the meeting.[7]

Dymond also inquired why Russo had not told the FBI or the Warren Commission about the assassination plans he had overheard. Russo answered: "At the time, right after the assassination, I had an involvement with school that was more pressing to me. If they wanted [to] ask me anything, they could."[8] He also said he didn't volunteer information about the conspiratorial meeting because the FBI indicated that Oswald was the lone assassin and, he added, "I had no reason to disagree with these people. They are professionals."[9] Moreover, he said, "Dave Ferrie was never implicated, as far as I knew."[10] Asked if he had heard of Garrison's investigation, Russo admitted that he had read about it in the newspapers and also that "David W. Ferrie was being investigated." "As a matter of fact," the defense counsel asked dramatically, "didn't you wait until Ferrie was dead so that there wouldn't be a witness to contradict your statement as to such a meeting as that?" Russo replied that he had not realized, when he read the story, that David W. Ferrie was the same person as the Dave Ferrie he knew because he "never knew his middle name was W."[11]

Russo also admitted under cross-examination that he had been hypnotized three times before the preliminary hearing—a method Garrison said he used in order to "objectify" testimony.[12] Moreover, it was learned that Russo had been under psychiatric treatment for eighteen months, ending in late 1960, and had last consulted a psychiatrist as recently as 1966.[13]

### The Prisoner

The District Attorney found his only other witness, Vernon B. Bundy, in the Orleans Parish Prison after the hearing had begun. Assistant District Attorney Charles Ray Ward and other members of Garrison's staff strenuously objected to using Bundy as a witness, but Garrison put him on the stand anyway.[14] Bundy, a narcotics addict and petty thief, testified that in the summer of 1963, while he was preparing to inject the contents of two capsules of heroin into his arm, he saw two men meet on the shore of Lake Pontchartrain, on the outskirts of New Orleans. One, whom Bundy described as "a junkie or beatnik type" with a light growth of beard, he had later recognized from photographs as Lee Harvey Oswald. The other man Bundy identified as Clay Shaw. Like Russo, Bundy had never before told anyone about his encounter with Oswald.[15] The three-judge panel ruled that there was sufficient evidence for a trial. The decision was by no means startling; it merely established that there was evidence that merited judgment. Yet to many people the ruling suggested that Garrison had won some sort of legal victory. A few days later, on March 22, the Orleans Parish Grand Jury, to which Jim Garrison is legal adviser, returned a formal indictment against Clay Shaw based on essentially the same evidence.[16]

## The Sciambra Memorandum

As it turned out, the evidence used at the preliminary hearing was even less sound than it may have appeared at the time. About six weeks after the hearing, James R. Phelan reported in the *Saturday Evening Post* that Russo had told two contradictory stories —one in his first interview with Sciambra, the other in court, after being questioned under hypnosis. Phelan discovered the discrepancy when Garrison, with his customary generosity to journalists, supplied him with a memorandum of Russo's first interview.[17] Nowhere in this document, which ran to thirty-five hundred words, was the supposed meeting among Shaw, Ferrie, and Oswald mentioned, either directly or implicitly. Yet two weeks later, in court, Russo stated that it had definitely taken place. In his first interview, moreover, Russo did not state that he had ever met Shaw, and he himself made no mention whatever of a Bertrand— either Clay or Clem. Assistant District Attorney Sciambra, who conducted this first interview and wrote up the memorandum, later said that Russo did tell him of the assassination plot but that he forgot to include it in his report. (Sciambra also stated that he had burned his original notes of the interview.)[18] Yet Sciambra's own words in the memorandum would appear to belie this explanation: "The next picture that he [Russo] identified was that of Clay Shaw. He said that he saw this man twice. The first time was when he pulled into Ferrie's service station to get his car fixed. Shaw was the person sitting in the compact car talking with Ferrie. He remembers seeing him again at the Nashville Street Wharf when he went to see J.F.K. speak."[19] Here Sciambra specifically states that Russo said he saw Shaw twice, and neither occasion involved a rendezvous in Ferrie's apartment during which Shaw, Ferrie, and Oswald planned the assassination. If Russo went on to describe a third encounter, and that was the only one relevant to Garrison's case, it is difficult to understand how Sciambra could have neglected to include it in the memorandum. Moreover, according to Billings, Sciambra did not mention the alleged "third encounter" in an oral report he made to Garrison the day after the interview. Sciambra reported that Russo said he had seen Shaw only twice

—once at Ferrie's service station and once at the Nashville Street Wharf. In fact, the first time Billings heard of the third encounter, during which Russo was supposed to have overheard Bertrand, Ferrie, and Oswald planning the assassination in Ferrie's apartment, was on February 27, two days before Shaw was arrested, when Sciambra himself *told* Russo that he had mentioned the name Bertrand and had described the meeting in Ferrie's apartment. This, it will be recalled, was after Russo had taken the "truth serum." And Russo still, at this time, said that he could not remember anyone named Bertrand.[20]

If a witness tells two contradictory stories, external evidence may make it possible to choose between them. In Russo's case, the corroborative evidence available casts doubt on his second story—the one he told in court. He testified that Oswald was Ferrie's roommate in early September 1963, yet there is evidence that at that time Oswald was living with his wife and their baby daughter on Magazine Street in New Orleans.[21] Russo described Oswald as having a beard in early and mid-September, yet generally reliable witnesses reported that Oswald was clean-shaven at that time.[22] Russo claimed that he saw Oswald in Ferrie's apartment in the first week of October, yet Oswald was known to have been in Mexico and Dallas during this period.[23] Russo said that a friend of his, Niles Peterson, was at a party at Ferrie's apartment the night that he saw Oswald and Shaw there, yet Peterson flatly denies that he saw anyone fitting the description of either Shaw or Oswald. (Peterson did, however, recall a bearded man who was six feet tall and otherwise fitted the description of the man who was known to be Ferrie's roommate at the time—James R. Lewallen.[24]) Russo claimed, further, that a young woman, Sandra Moffitt, accompanied him to Ferrie's apartment the night of the meeting, yet she denies this, and says that she did not meet Ferrie until 1964.[25] In sum, Russo's court testimony appears to be at odds with a great many of the external points of reference he himself provided.

## Hypnosis

A transcript of Russo's first hypnosis session, which Garrison also gave to Phelan, reveals that many of the details of Russo's story were developed under hypnosis.[26] Russo was hypnotized on March 2, the day after Clay Shaw was arrested, by a Dr. Esmond Fatter, who told him to imagine a television screen in his mind. "You are in Ferrie's apartment," Dr. Fatter said. "Look at the picture and tell us the story that you see." Russo talked about some of Ferrie's friends but said nothing about an assassination plot or conspiratorial meeting.[27] Dr. Fatter then probed deeper, saying, "Now picture the screen again, Perry, and it is a picture of Ferrie's apartment, and there are several people in there and there is a white-haired man. Tell me about it." Russo described a party at Ferrie's apartment in which "everybody is drinking beer"; but again he did not mention anything about an assassination plot.[28] Then Dr. Fatter instructed Russo to let his "mind go completely blank" and again "notice the picture on the television screen." Dr. Fatter suggested,

"There will be Bertrand, Ferrie and Oswald and they are going to discuss a very important matter and there is another man and girl there and they are talking about assassinating somebody. Look at it and describe it to me." The story that Russo then told is similar to the one he told in court about overhearing an assassination plot.[29]

Although Garrison said that hypnosis was part of his "objectifying machinery,"[30] and that he expected it to be "hailed as an unprecedented step in jurisprudence,"[31] Dr. Jay Katz, a professor of both law and clinical psychology at Yale University, expressed some severe reservations about it. After reading the transcripts of Russo's hypnotic sessions, Dr. Katz said that in his opinion "the hypnotist introduced very leading questions." "This was most striking," Dr. Katz continued, "when he directly asked him, or in fact told him, to tell him about the conversation that took place in respect to an assassination plot." Moreover, Dr. Katz said that under hypnosis many subjects have difficulty differentiating between fact and fantasy.[32]

After the preliminary hearing, Russo began showing doubts about his identification of Shaw. He told James Phelan, who had spent more than forty hours questioning him for his *Saturday Evening Post* article, that he wished he could have an "opportunity to talk to Shaw for a few hours so I can be sure he was the right man."[33] He told Richard Townley, a reporter for WDSU-TV, in New Orleans, that he was unsure of his testimony and, according to Townley, said it was difficult for him now to distinguish "reality and fantasy."[34]

The testimony of Garrison's other witness, Vernon

Bundy, also raised a number of questions. One of Bundy's fellow-inmates in the Parish Prison, Miguel Torres, told an NBC interviewer that Bundy had admitted to him that he was testifying for Garrison "because it's the only way that I can get cut loose"— indicating that unless he did testify, his probation would be revoked and he would have to complete a five-year sentence in prison. Bundy was subsequently arrested on a charge of robbery. Another inmate, John (the Baptist) Cancler, said in an interview that Bundy had told him that his account of the events at Lake Pontchartrain was a fabrication.[35] Of course, felons are not known for their probity, and Garrison dismissed the statements of Torres and Cancler "in view of their criminal records." But if no credence is to be placed in the testimony of Bundy's fellow-convicts, what of the testimony of Bundy himself?

Garrison's entire case at the preliminary hearing, then, was based on the allegations of two witnesses who had both waited four years before disclosing uncorroborated stories and who both subsequently cast considerable doubt on their own testimony.

### A Case of Perjury

A few months after the hearing, there was another legal skirmish that strengthened the appearance, if not the substance, of Garrison's case: Dean Andrews, the New Orleans lawyer who had claimed that shortly after the assassination a shadowy figure named Clay Bertrand appealed to him to go to Dallas and defend Oswald, became involved in perjury proceedings. Andrews, after telling a number of stories about Bertrand, and at one point, it will be recalled, claiming that Bertrand was a figment of his imagination, was called before the Orleans Parish Grand Jury in March 1967. Asked if Clay Shaw was Clay Bertrand, he replied, under oath, "I can't say that he is and I can't say that he ain't."[36] Three months later, on June 28, Andrews volunteered to appear again before the grand jury. This time, he told of a "deal" he had made with Garrison not to say categorically that Clay Shaw was *not* Clay Bertrand, even though, he testified, he never thought for a moment that Clay Shaw was Clay Bertrand. Bertrand, he admitted, was a fictitious name he had used in order to protect a friend of his, a bartender in the French Quarter. Andrews acknowledged that he had perjured himself previously, and said, "It doesn't make any difference to me if I'm convicted. . . . Clay Shaw is not Clay Bertrand. Indict me if you want to."[37]

When Andrews was subsequently arraigned, tried, and convicted for perjury, Garrison declared that this represented "a major conviction . . . in connection with this case."[38] It was, if anything, a Pyrrhic victory. Assistant District Attorney Alcock charged at the trial that the name Bertrand had been "foisted on the world" by Andrews,[39] but if Bertrand was indeed a fiction, invented by Andrews after the assassination, how could Russo testify that he had met Shaw before the assassination under the pseudonym Bertrand? According to the Sciambra memorandum, Russo had not mentioned the name Bertrand in his initial interview. It was only after Sciambra told Russo that he had identified one of the participants at the meeting in Ferrie's apartment as Bertrand while Russo was under the influence of sodium pentothal—an identification which, according to Billings, Russo did not recall at the time—and after Russo was allowed to ask leading questions about the case so that, in his own words, he "could figure out what they wanted to know," that the name Bertrand found its way into his story.

In what may well turn out to be a self-fulfilling prophecy, Garrison has predicted that the case of Clay Shaw "will never be permitted to come to trial."[40] According to the Louisiana code of criminal procedure, the district attorney is empowered to fix the date of a trial (which then must be approved by the Court), and thus has effective control over the docket, or schedule of cases. Despite Garrison's announcements on several occasions that a date had been set for the trial of Clay Shaw, an examination of the court records shows that—as of October 1968—no date for the trial has ever been actually scheduled by the District Attorney since the arrest of Shaw in March 1967.[41] This is no doubt partly due to the somewhat unusual procedure Garrison followed in arresting Shaw: instead of waiting until he had obtained sufficient evidence for a court trial, Garrison, it will be recalled, arrested Shaw on the basis of an unsubstantiated (and altered) story of a single witness, and then, *after* arresting Shaw, sought evidence that would corroborate the story in court.[42] The trial was further delayed by the defense, which held that the numerous public statements Garrison had made about the case created an atmosphere in New Orleans prejudicial to the defendant,

and asked for a change of venue. (Garrison added to
this delay by filing a token protest against the Court's
decision to hear the defense's motions.)[43] Finally,
Shaw's attorneys asked a federal court to intervene on
the ground that Garrison had conducted "a reign of
terror by the misuse and abuse of the powers of the
public office" and thus had denied the defendant the
possibility of obtaining a fair trial.[44] Although a
three-judge federal court in Louisiana denied this plea,
it ordered Garrison not to proceed with the case until
the appeal of this motion could be heard by the United
States Supreme Court.[45] Both sides expressed doubts at
the time that the case would ever come to trial,[46] but in
December 1968 the Supreme Court refused to intervene,
and said that Louisiana may proceed. Garrison, in turn,
announced plans to try the case early in 1969.[47]

# IV

## The Search

If it takes me thirty years to nail every one of the assassins, then I will continue this investigation for thirty years.

—Jim Garrison in *Playboy*

After the preliminary hearing, there was a second notable shift in the nature of the investigation. Whereas the first phase had concentrated on the activities of David Ferrie, and the second was devoted principally to efforts to substantiate Russo's allegations about Clay Shaw, the third phase had no single specific objective. It was, in effect, a hunt without a quarry, a search for any information from any source that might relate to any aspect of the assassination. For this desultory pursuit, Garrison reinforced his permanent staff with volunteer recruits from the growing corps of critics of the Warren Commission. A number of these people who might best be described as peripatetic demonologists found in New Orleans an unexpected rallying point; they were attracted to Garrison like the children of Hamelin to the Pied Piper. At the head of the line stood Mark Lane, the author of *Rush to Judgment,* who, together with William Turner, the *Ramparts* writer, spent months assiduously combing Garrison's files on the case for new clues and devising ingenious schemes to produce new disclosures. (When one assistant district attorney protested that by making Xerox copies of the evidence Lane might be jeopardizing the case, Garrison replied that Lane and Turner were "writing the official history of the investigation.")[1] Reports on developments in Texas came from Penn Jones, Jr., the crusading editor of the Midlothian, Texas, *Mirror* and the author of a series of booklets called "Forgive My Grief," the most celebrated feature of which was a death count of individuals who were even peripherally connected with the assassination, and from Allan Chapman, a knight-errant in a two-hundred-year-old crusade against the Illuminati (supposedly a worldwide conspiracy of intellectuals who now control the television networks). Harold Weisberg, the author of a numerically consecutive series of books called *Whitewash,* was charged with the task of going through the twenty-six volumes of the Warren Commission's testimony and evidence for new leads relevant to Garrison's investigation. Two specialists in photographic interpretation, Raymond Marcus and Richard Sprague, scanned films of the assassination to detect previously neglected pieces that might fit into what Garrison calls his "jigsaw puzzle." Three trouble-shooters-at-large also assisted—Vincent Salandria, a lawyer from Philadelphia; Richard H. Popkin, a professor of philosophy at the University of California at San Diego and the author of "The Second Oswald," a conjectural essay originally published in the *New York Review of Books* which suggests that the assassination was performed not by Oswald but by his *Doppelgänger*; and the night-club and television comedian Mort Sahl.[2] Although these amateur sleuths, who sometimes referred to themselves as the Dealey Plaza Irregulars, provided Garrison with the bulk of the new "evidence" that he cited in numerous public appearances—including a coast-to-coast tour of radio and television shows in connection with the *Playboy* interview—they occasionally proved a source of friction for the professional investigators on Garrison's staff.

Thomas Bethell, who worked on the investigation as a member of Garrison's staff since its inception, described the contribution of the amateurs this way: "The trouble with these third-rate students is that the only way they can make a strong impression on Garrison is by coming up with flamboyant nonsense, thus hoping to be hired as someone with original ideas. They therefore represent a serious threat to the sanity of the investigation. One of them has a bad habit of steering Garrison into crackpot directions, such as the 'Storm Drain Theory,' to which Garrison tends to be susceptible."[3] And the more parvenu experts advocated a certain "original idea," the more susceptible Garrison apparently became. When Allan Chapman, the Illuminati specialist, lent his support to the theory that a shot had been fired from a storm drain in Dealey Plaza that day in Dallas,[4] Garrison stated on television that the bullet that killed President Kennedy was "fired by a man standing in a sewer manhole."[5] Thus, Garrison added a sixteenth man to the team that he claims carried out the assassination and a fifth spot from which he has said the shots were fired. Six months before, Garrison had theorized that there were only two assassins—one, Oswald, in the Texas School Book Depository building and one on the so-called grassy knoll, just beyond the building and on the same side of the street.[6] After discussing the case with Weisberg, who believes that there was another rifleman in the nearby Dal-Tex building, Garrison accommodatingly added a third rifleman there, and also exonerated Oswald from having fired any of the shots.[7] Then Marcus came along with a blowup of some trees and shadows on the grassy knoll, claiming that this revealed some figures concealed in the bushes, and Garrison added four more assassins to the band. (Two of them, he has suggested, were there to pick up stray cartridge cases.)[8] Next, the independent investigator Jones Harris showed Garrison a blowup of a truck parked behind a picket fence, and the "commando team" grew by two.[9] By mid-June 1967, Garrison was saying that the assassination was performed by a fourteen-man team of Cuban guerrilla fighters.[10] Finally, after discussing the matter at some length with Professor Popkin, Garrison posited a "second Oswald," who was sent to impersonate the first Oswald at the scene.[11] (This understandably disconcerted some members of his staff, since the presence of a second Oswald would tend to vitiate the legal case against Clay Shaw: did Shaw conspire with Oswald, as he is accused of doing, or with an impersonator?)[12] The assassins were supported, according to Garrison, by Jack Ruby and some members of the Dallas Police Department.[13]

Although the exact number of assassins changed from one public statement to the next, the "forces behind the conspiracy" grew steadily. In the early stages of the investigation, Garrison had told Senator Russell Long that only a few insignificant men were involved.[14] Then, after Ferrie's death, Garrison began to specify the guilty parties, identifying them as a band of perverts and anti-Castro Cubans. With the arrival of the demonologists, however, the conspiracy was rapidly escalated to include Minutemen,[15] CIA agents,[16] oil millionaires,[17] Dallas policemen,[18] munitions exporters,[19] "the Dallas Establishment,"[20] reactionaries,[21] White Russians,[22] and certain elements of "the invisible Nazi substructure."[23]

On what sort of evidence was this extraordinary conspiracy predicated? Garrison's method of deducing the last member of the team is perhaps indicative. The figure of what may be reckoned as the sixteenth assassin was extrapolated from two newspaper photographs taken about ten minutes after the assassination. The first shows a man in a dark suit apparently examining a curb near the spot where President Kennedy was shot, with two policemen shown looking on. Garrison claimed on a television program that he could detect in this photograph a pebble-like object partly concealed by the heavily matted grass, and he stated that this object is a .45-caliber bullet "which killed John Kennedy, which has markings on it that would show [that] the automatic gun from which it came [was a] handgun."[24] The bullet is not readily visible to the naked eye; in fact, according

to one member of Garrison's staff, the photograph is so
grainy that it is impossible to be certain that the
pebble-like object is not in fact a pebble.[25] The other
photograph, taken seconds later, shows the man in
the dark suit walking away with his hands closed.
Flashing this photograph in front of television cameras
in Dallas, Garrison declared that the man (from his
appearance Garrison somehow surmised him to be a
"federal agent") had "got the bullet clutched in his
hand, the bullet that killed John Kennedy."[26] Garrison never explained how he could determine from a
photograph that a bullet was being held in a man's
closed fist—and even discern its calibre. However, this
was the "evidence" that Garrison cited in support of
the theory that an assassin was in a sewer, and of his
own charge on television that "the bullet which killed
John Kennedy, which fell in the grass with pieces of
the President's head, was in the hands of the federal
government ten minutes after the President was dead."
And Garrison went even further. "This means that the
federal government knowingly participated in framing
Lee Oswald," he said. "Lyndon Johnson had to know
this."[27] Garrison himself, however, eliminated this assassin in the sewer in his later press statements; for
example, in his July 11, 1968, press conference he
listed the "shooting points" as the "Dal-Tex building,"
the "Dallas Book Depository building," and the "grassy
knoll."[28]

Although most of the assassins were identified only
as projections of connected dots in enlargements of
photographs of trees and shrubbery, the man whom
Garrison identified in *Playboy* as the seventh member

of the assassination team turned out, much to the District Attorney's embarrassment, to be a real person. Garrison alleged that this seventh man "created a diversionary action in order to distract people's attention from the snipers," explaining, "This individual screamed, fell to the ground, and simulated an epileptic fit, drawing people away from the vicinity of the knoll just before the President's motorcade reached the ambush point."[29] Garrison further described this man, presumably one of a number of anti-Castro Cuban paramilitarists, as being clad in green combat fatigues.[30] As it happened, however, the person Garrison was talking about was Jerry Boyd Belknap, an employee of the *Dallas News*, who had fainted in Dealey Plaza about twenty minutes before the motorcade arrived. Belknap explained to the FBI that he had had frequent fainting spells since suffering a serious head injury in an automobile accident in 1960, and that he had been receiving daily medication to prevent these spells.[31] When Garrison learned in June 1967 that the man who fainted was not the paramilitarist he had presumed him to be, he told his staff to forget about the matter.[32] Yet in his public statements he continued to say that he had located this seventh member of the commando team.[*][33]

A prosecutor who wants to insure that the story of his investigation remains newsworthy must produce new evidence constantly. Garrison's corps of Irregulars proved helpful not simply in digging out new evidence but, on occasion, in finding opportunities for Garrison

---

[*] According to Bethell, Garrison had the FBI report on Belknap before he made the statement in *Playboy* about the "diversionary action."

to present it. When Mort Sahl appeared on the Johnny Carson television show in January 1968 and complained about the coverage that the various media had given the District Attorney and his case, Carson agreed to have Garrison on his program, provided that he would not merely reiterate old charges but would present new evidence. Garrison telegraphed Carson accepting the impromptu offer. And on the evening of January 31, Carson devoted most of his show to an interview with Garrison. When Carson asked Garrison to reveal the new evidence that he claimed he had, Garrison reached into a black leather portfolio he held in his lap and pulled out some photographs, which, he said, showed suspects being arrested immediately after the assassination. "Here are the pictures of five of them being arrested," he said, "and they've never been shown before." He went on to say, "Several of these men arrested have been connected by our office with the Central Intelligence Agency."[34] The new evidence Garrison presented that night had been found by Allan Chapman some weeks before, in the photographic department of the Dallas *Times Herald*. Robert Hollingsworth, managing editor of the *Times Herald*, has told me that he personally inspected with a magnifying glass the photographs given to Chapman, and that they showed nothing more than some bystanders, two of whom were employed in the building in which Oswald worked, being routinely questioned by policemen. (Police reports included in the Warren Commission's published evidence [Volume XIX, Decker Exhibits] indicate that a number of individuals were also taken into custody in the confusion after the shooting, and possibly some were photographed.) Carson, who was, of course, seeing the pictures for the first time, had no way of knowing who the individuals in the pictures were or whether they were in fact "being arrested," and he had no way of challenging Garrison's claim that they were connected with the CIA. What Garrison presented to the public that night, then, was not actually new evidence—witnesses pictured in his photographs had testified before the Warren Commission—but a new and totally unsubstantiated interpretation of old evidence.

Any sensational murder case attracts its share of crank letters, publicity seekers, and bogus tips, and, whereas most district attorneys regard such offers of help as a nuisance, Garrison found them a rich source of new witnesses, ready to provide allegations and disclosures of the sort required to keep his story current in the press. Although it is extremely doubtful whether any of these volunteer witnesses will ever testify in court, the case of a man named Donald Philetus Norton illustrates the use to which the testimony of such "secret witnesses" can be put in the open arena of public opinion. Norton, a thirty-four-year-old night-club entertainer, got in touch with Garrison in June 1967, claiming that he had been a CIA courier, and that he had delivered fifty thousand dollars to a man who was "a dead ringer for Oswald" in Mexico in 1962 and had received a hundred-and-fifty-thousand-dollar "pickup" from David Ferrie in 1958. He said, further, that he would like to work as an investigator for Garrison. Norton[35] was immediately brought to New Orleans from Vancouver, where he was living at the time, and was interrogated by Garrison's still-pseudonymous intelligence expert Bill Boxley. Though Norton was more than willing to identify Oswald, Ferrie, and even Shaw as CIA agents, his story contained so many contradictions and implausibilities that Boxley and other staff members concluded that he would be totally ineffective as a witness. (It was later revealed that he was a convicted bank embezzler with a prison record.) But even though Norton was turned down in July as a possible court witness, Garrison referred to him as a "secret witness" in the interview that appeared in the October 1967 issue of *Playboy*. "We have evidence that Oswald maintained his CIA contacts . . . and that Ferrie was also employed by the CIA," he announced. "In this regard, we will present in court a witness—formerly a CIA courier—who met both Ferrie and Oswald officially in their CIA connection."[36] This "courier" was later identified by a member of Garrison's staff as Norton.[37]

Another witness found in the mail—this one with Professor Popkin's help—was Richard C. Nagell, then confined in the psychiatric section of the Medical Center for Federal Prisoners in Springfield, Missouri. Nagell had been arrested while attempting to rob a bank in El Paso in September 1963. After the assassination, he claimed that he had purposely got himself arrested in order to provide an alibi because he had had advance knowledge of the assassination conspiracy; his part in it, according to Garrison, had been to kill Oswald, who was the "patsy."[38] Although Nagell was a convicted felon, whose own defense had raised questions about his mental status, Garrison thought his story worth pursuing and sent a former assistant district attorney, William R. Martin, to Missouri to interview him. Nagell insisted he had proof of the conspiracy in the form of tape recordings. When these could not be found, Nagell told Martin, "They've stolen the tapes," and refused to discuss the matter any further. Though Nagell, like Norton, was finally rejected by Garrison as a court witness, the District Attorney continued to use Nagell's story to bolster his case in public. Explaining Oswald's role as a patsy, Garrison stated in *Playboy*, "We have evidence that the plan was to have him [Oswald] shot as a cop killer in the Texas Theater 'while resisting arrest.'" Garrison said he was unable to divulge the evidence at the time, but the whole thing was one of Nagell's tales.[39] (Nagell was later released from prison and claimed that Garrison's investigator, Martin, was himself a CIA agent and distorted his story.)

Another confidential witness with whom Garrison spent a good deal of time is a Dallas ex-convict who has been under suspicion in Texas for attempted murder. According to Thomas Bethell, this witness "drops into the office at fairly frequent intervals and readily identifies almost anyone you show him a photograph of."[40] He proved more co-operative than accurate. Of thirteen new witnesses found through the mail or with the help of the Irregulars assisting Garrison, nearly all have turned out to have criminal records or to have been under psychiatric care.

To facilitate the publication of his *Playboy* interview, Garrison provided the editors of the magazine with "secret evidence" which, he claimed, was to be used in his court case and was "not for publica-cation."[41] Subsequently, however, Gordon Novel, who was mentioned quite prominently in the interview, sued *Playboy* for libel, and in the course of the pre-trial litigation the memorandum containing Garrison's "secret evidence" was examined by Elmer Gertz, Novel's attorney, and entered into the court record.[42] Virtually all of the "secret evidence" consists of un-corroborated allegations of volunteer witnesses. For example, one item in the memorandum states, "Garri-son has a witness, Raymond Cummings [a Dallas taxicab driver], who will testify that he saw Oswald, Shaw and Ruby together in Dallas on one occasion and Oswald and Ruby on another." According to Bethell, Shaw was not mentioned in Cummings' story,[43] and furthermore Garrison himself told James D. Squires, a reporter for the *Nashville Tennesseean*, that he was not using Cummings as a witness.[44] Another court witness Garrison cited in the memorandum was Clyde Johnson, who, Garrison claimed, would testify in court that Clay Shaw and Lee Harvey Oswald had visited him in a Baton Rouge hotel room in 1963 and offered him six thousand dollars to denounce Kennedy for his "betrayal" of Cuba. Johnson had in fact given Garrison's office a statement to that effect on March 30, 1967, but when it turned out that Oswald was in Mexico on the day that Johnson had claimed he had visited his hotel room, Johnson said on a local radio program that he would not repeat his testimony in court, even if he had to take the Fifth Amendment.[45] Again, although his witness had been effectively dis-qualified as a court witness, Garrison still found some

use for him as a "secret witness." A third item in the
memorandum states that "Garrison has two other witnesses who will testify that Shaw and Oswald met together in several small Louisiana towns in the summer
and fall of 1963." The witnesses referred to were two
itinerant mural artists, Mr. and Mrs. Cedric Younger
Von Rolleston, who appeared in Garrison's office in July
1967 and claimed that they had seen Clay Shaw with
Lee Harvey Oswald in the Bentley Hotel in Alexandria,
Louisiana, in October 1963.[46] Subsequently, the Von
Rollestons went to the offices of Clay Shaw's lawyers,
and requested to see Clay Shaw, then, after meeting
with Shaw, swore in an affidavit that they had never
before met Shaw and that the identification they had
made earlier from photographs in Garrison's office was
incorrect.[47] Evidence like this was of course far more
effective as "secret evidence," which could be presented confidentially to journalists and editors, than
as court evidence.

The "mailbag," as all the unsolicited tips and offers
to testify were called around the District Attorney's
office, also provided Garrison with data for his public
statements. For example, after receiving an anonymous
letter suggesting that President Kennedy might have
been shot with "frangible" (or dumdum) bullets,[48]
Garrison asserted in his *Playboy* interview that "some
of the gunmen appear to have used frangible bullets."[49] And it also led to one arrest. William Turner
(the *Ramparts* staff writer and former FBI employee)
ran across a letter alleging that a Californian named
Eugene Bradley had once made inflammatory comments on President Kennedy. Investigating the matter,

Turner found an Edgar Eugene Bradley, who raised funds for a radio program called "20th Century Reformation Hour," and who happened to have been in Texas on the day of the assassination—though in El Paso, not in Dallas. On the basis of this information, Garrison, who at the time was in Los Angeles raising funds himself, telephoned his office in New Orleans and ordered Assistant District Attorney Alcock to issue a warrant for Bradley's arrest, charging him with conspiracy to kill President Kennedy. Bethell reported concern among the staff members; there was nothing in the files on Bradley except the letter, and no one in the office had even heard of Bradley as a suspect. The warrant was issued anyway, and Bradley was arrested in Los Angeles and then released in his own recognizance. When Garrison returned to New Orleans, he explained to his bewildered staff that he had further investigated Bradley, but saw little prospect of his ever being extradited by Governor Ronald Reagan.[50] This became another one of Garrison's self-fulfilling prophecies. In November 1968, California refused extradition because Garrison had failed to produce any witnesses to substantiate the charges against Bradley.[51] After he had left Garrison's staff, William Gurvich said, "Jim has a philosophy about national headlines. He believes that everyone reads the headlines concerning arrests and charges but few people read denials or correcting statements."[52]

# V

# The Thousand-Pound Canary

To read the press accounts of my investigation—
my "circus," I should say—I'm a cross between Al
Capone and Attila the Hun, ruthlessly hounding
innocent men, trampling their legal rights, bribing
and threatening witnesses, and in general violating
every canon of legal ethics.

—Jim Garrison in *Playboy*

American district attorneys enjoy a pre-eminent control over the administration of justice in their respec-
tive bailiwicks. They have the power to initiate or to
terminate investigations, to decide which cases finally
to prosecute and which to quash, and, in effect, to
adjudicate penalties in advance of trial by negotiating
with the defense counsel over a defendant's plea. Institutional constraints on such powers are minimal.
As Raymond Moley has long since demonstrated in
his classic study *Politics and Criminal Prosecution*, a
grand jury, which theoretically acts as the primary
check on the discretion of a district attorney, tends
in fact to become little more than a rubber stamp for
his actions; the members of the grand jury are, after

all, only laymen, whereas the prosecutor is a trained lawyer, and the decisions which the grand jury renders are almost exclusively structured by the prosecutor's own presentation of evidence and argument.[1] In Orleans Parish, the district attorney has the additional advantage of being able to subpoena witnesses peremptorily without having to consult the grand jury, and he may even bring persons to trial, by-passing the usual process of grand-jury indictment, merely by signing what is known as a "bill of information" against them; moreover, it is part of his official responsibility to serve as legal adviser to the same grand jury which is supposed to check *his* legal powers.

In the objections which the mass media have from time to time raised against Garrison and his methods, however, seldom have they focused on any questionable use of these legitimate powers of the District Attorney's office. Rather, it has become customary to criticize Garrison for resorting to extralegal means of conducting his investigation. Charges of bribery, in particular, have been frequently leveled against Garrison and his staff, and many of these have received prominent coverage in the press and on television. In June 1967, for instance, it was widely reported that Miguel Torres, the former drug addict who was then an inmate at the Louisiana State Prison at Angola, was alleging that Garrison had arranged to have him transferred to the Orleans Parish Prison and had offered him both a parole and a supply of heroin if he would agree to submit to hypnosis and then testify against Clay Shaw—this despite Torres' insistence that he had never known Shaw.[2] At the same time, John Cancler—

the Parish Prison inmate who had debunked Vernon
Bundy's testimony at the preliminary hearing in March
1967—claimed that a representative of Garrison's staff
had offered to drop the burglary charges then pending against him if he would agree to plant a piece of
incriminating evidence in Clay Shaw's home.[3] In the
NBC critique of Garrison's case, Sandra Moffitt, Perry
Russo's acquaintance, appeared to say that she had
been offered gifts of "clothing" and certain other "considerations" in return for her co-operation with Garrison's office.[4] On the same broadcast, Fred Lemanns,
sometime operator of a New Orleans Turkish bath,
alleged that Garrison had offered to help finance a
"private club" for him if he would sign a statement to
the effect that he had seen Shaw in the company of
Lee Harvey Oswald in the bathhouse of his establishment. (Lemanns went on to say that he finally did
sign the statement, even though he knew it to be
false.)[5] And *Newsweek*, in its critical report, quoted
Alvin Beauboeuf, whom David Ferrie had designated
in his will as the sole heir to his estate, who stated
that one of Garrison's investigators had offered to pay
him three thousand dollars if he would supply testimony to support the case against Shaw.[6]

Garrison himself seems to have taken such charges
in stride. "Like every police department and district
attorney's office across the country," he once explained,
"we have sums set aside to pay informers for valuable
information—but we would never suborn perjury."[7]
And he chided the mass media for making so much
of the allegations of attempted subornation made by
these various witnesses. "It's rather naïve," he said,

"apart from being ethically objectionable, to assume that our investigators travel around the country with bags of money trying to bribe witnesses to lie on the witness stand. We just don't operate that way."[8]

Regardless of whether Garrison's office indeed operated "that way," it is true that his critics appeared unduly preoccupied with the business of exposing such blatantly unscrupulous practices as bribery and subornation of perjury. By concentrating on these sensational charges, reporters generally neglected to reveal the District Attorney's more subtle uses of those substantial powers invested in his office—legitimate powers to be sure, but ones which may be exercised with no less unscrupulous intent. According to Gurvich, it was a "real education" to see how the District Attorney would apply various pressures to individuals whom he identified as "potential witnesses." Gurvich points to the case of Morris Brownlee, the godson of David Ferrie, whom Garrison once had arrested on a narcotics charge. Though that charge had been dropped earlier by Garrison for lack of evidence, when Garrison became interested in Ferrie and his possible involvement in an assassination conspiracy, he had Brownlee arrested again on the same charge, then brought Ferrie in to see his godson in jail and offered once again to quash the charges if Ferrie would "co-operate" with him.[9] Gurvich describes Garrison's typical *modus operandi* this way: first he would befriend "potential witnesses"; then, after obtaining some leading information or incriminating statements, he would proceed to "put the screws on them"; and when the witness had no other alternative open to him, Garrison would offer to make some sort of "deal" for the witness's "co-operation."[10] Garrison's treatment of Dean Andrews, the jive-talking lawyer who first brought the name of Clay Bertrand to his attention and whom he subsequently had convicted of perjury, represents a telling case in point.

### Dean Andrews

Some time in the fall of 1966, Jim Garrison invited Dean Andrews, a long-standing acquaintance who was then an assistant district attorney in neighboring Jefferson Parish, to have dinner with him at Broussard's. As Andrews tells it, Garrison seemed especially concerned with the fact that "Oswald was on his turf a few months before he assassinated Number One." Since Oswald had come to Andrews seeking legal advice during his stay in New Orleans, Garrison was interested in knowing something of Andrews' impressions of Oswald. The two men "kicked a few theories about the assassination around," Andrews said, and then "the Green Giant mooched my copy of the Warren Report because he didn't even own a copy then."[11] A few weeks later, Garrison informed Andrews that he was "reopening" the investigation into the assassination of President Kennedy, and he asked Andrews for his assistance. Specifically, he wanted information on three individuals: David Ferrie, whom Garrison called the "getaway pilot"; the unidentified stocky Mexican man who, Andrews had previously told the Warren Commission, had accompanied Oswald to his office; and Clay Bertrand, the individual who Andrews testified had called him shortly after the assassination and had asked him to defend Oswald in Dallas. But Andrews was able to supply Garrison with little more than the old leads he had already furnished the Warren Commission. He told the District Attorney what has been reported earlier: that his only contact with David Ferrie had occurred when he arranged a parole for one of Ferrie's friends, an action which, he acknowledged, "was not a strictly legal move for an assistant D.A. to make." As for the mysterious Mexican and Clay Bertrand, Andrews told Garrison that he knew the former only as "Oswald's shadow" and the latter as no more than the "voice on the phone."[12]

Shortly before Christmas, Garrison and Andrews had a second dinner meeting. Andrews recalls that Garrison had come up with the theory that "Clay Bertrand" was in fact a pseudonym for Clay Shaw. According to Andrews, he insisted that Garrison was mistaken, that Clay Shaw was not "in any way, shape or form, Clay Bertrand." In subsequent meetings, however, Garrison persisted in theorizing that Clay Shaw and Clay Bertrand were one and the same; and Garrison, in Andrews' words, "attempted to brainwash me" into identifying Shaw as Bertrand. Andrews claims that he was growing increasingly suspicious of Garrison's tactics, especially in view of this obstinate identification of Bertrand as Shaw. As a means of testing Garrison's probity, Andrews says, he dropped "two bum names— 'Mannie Garcia Gonzales' and 'Ricardo Davis' "—men whom he identified for the District Attorney as "Cuban guerrilla fighters." Andrews indicates that he had fabricated both names "out of my head on the spur of the moment . . . to see if the Giant's kosher."[13] A few days later Andrews decided his suspicions were justified. Garrison announced that he had identified the "triggerman" in the assassination plot as "Manuel Garcia Gonzales"; he noted that a certain Emanuel Gonzales had been arrested earlier that year on a charge of carrying a concealed weapon, and he cited this fact as further evidence of his being on the right trail. (Gonzales is hardly an uncommon name among Latin Americans, and Garrison neglected to state what specific connection there was between the man who had carried a concealed weapon in New Orleans and the man who pulled the trigger in Dallas.) Andrews went to Garrison and told him that he had "the right ta-ta but the wrong ho-ho"—that is, the wrong Gonzales. The working relationship between Andrews and Garrison was beginning to deteriorate into a condition of mutual mistrust.[14]

Late in February of 1967, a few days before the arrest of Clay Shaw, Garrison asked Andrews to meet him for dinner once again. He told Andrews that he now had further evidence of Shaw's involvement in the assassination conspiracy, and he requested that Andrews remain silent on the Clay Bertrand matter until he had a chance to build the case against Shaw. Should he have failed to co-operate, Andrews claims, Garrison threatened to send him "to the Bastille." Andrews says that they finally worked out a "deal" whereby he would agree to avoid saying that Clay Shaw was definitely *not* Clay Bertrand. Andrews maintains that he yielded to the District Attorney's demands on the point because, if he refused, "the Jolly Green Giant would pounce on me like a thousand-pound canary."[15]

On March 1, 1967, Clay Shaw was arrested. In the application for a search warrant of Shaw's premises, it was stated that a "confidential informant" had heard "Clay Shaw (alias Clay Bertrand) . . . agree to kill John F. Kennedy." As had been the case with "Emanuel Gonzales," another of the names for which Andrews knew himself to be the District Attorney's original source, Garrison had again put his finger on "the wrong ho-ho"—the wrong man. Andrews claims that he found the "key" to just what Garrison was up to when the District Attorney "busted Clay Shaw as Clay Bertrand —and there ain't no such animal."[16]

The next day Andrews was subpoenaed to appear at the District Attorney's office; again he was asked about Clay Bertrand. In accordance with the deal he had previously made with Garrison, Andrews avoided saying directly that Shaw was not Bertrand. On March 9, a few days before Clay Shaw's preliminary hearing was scheduled to start, Andrews was summoned before the Orleans Parish Grand Jury. He was asked only to give his name, address, and occupation. Andrews himself describes this as another of Garrison's "tricks." "Once you go in front of the grand jury," he explains, "you can't open your mouth or tell anybody what happened in there. . . . If you do, you're subject to be penalized for contempt of court and prosecuted." In other words, by means of the grand-jury subpoena,

Garrison had effectively silenced Andrews, the only witness who could say for sure that Clay Shaw was *not* Clay Bertrand.[17]

After Shaw's preliminary hearing was completed, and the defendant was ordered to stand trial, Andrews was again called before the Orleans Parish Grand Jury. He was directed to state under oath whether or not Clay Shaw was the person whom he knew as Clay Bertrand. He answered, as he had agreed to, "I can't say that he is and I can't say he ain't."[18] Andrews was also asked whether he had ever arranged a parole for anyone on behalf of David Ferrie during his tenure as assistant district attorney in Jefferson Parish; he answered that he had not. If he had replied in the affirmative, acknowledging the information he had confidentially given Garrison several months before, he would have risked incriminating himself for having got a parole for a private client. Andrews was also questioned about statements he had previously made in the District Attorney's office, and was then indicted on five counts of perjury. Afterward, Andrews commented, "The Jolly Green Giant seeks out and destroys or cripples his enemies. . . . If you think a district attorney's subpoena isn't raw power, and if you think a district attorney's ability to present a matter to a grand jury and recommend, and interpret the law, isn't raw power, then you just don't know what goes on."[19]

As the case against Clay Shaw progressed, it became apparent to Andrews that Shaw was "just a poor unfortunate who was grabbed out of the sky by the

Jolly Green Giant, and his wizards and practitioners of voodoo, labeled Clay Bertrand, and bang, he's been tagged 'it' ever since." Andrews saw that his deal with Garrison was being used to "put the hat on" Clay Shaw—that is, to frame him.[20] In what he claims was an effort to undo this wrong, Andrews voluntarily appeared before the grand jury for a third time on June 28. He testified that he had known all along that Clay Shaw was not Clay Bertrand, the fictitious name which he said he had invented in order to protect the identity of his bartender friend. Furthermore, he acknowledged that he had previously told the grand jury that he was unable to say that Shaw was *not* Bertrand only because of the deal he had made with Garrison. For confessing this, and also in consequence of his earlier refusal to incriminate himself when he denied that he had arranged the parole for Ferrie's friend, Andrews was finally convicted of perjury.[21]

Thus, deftly using the legitimate powers of his office, Garrison had managed to discredit the one witness who could have undermined his court case by testifying that Clay Bertrand did not exist. (A convicted perjurer cannot testify in court in Louisiana.) And he succeeded as well in hoodwinking most of the press; few, if any, reporters and commentators seemed to recognize how the fact of Andrews' conviction tended to undermine rather than sustain the case against Clay Shaw. Though it was broadly reported that Garrison was hailing Andrews' conviction as a "major victory," what was not reported was the larger implication of Andrews' perjury: Andrews had in fact been convicted precisely because he admitted that Clay Shaw, the man whom

Garrison had arrested as Clay Bertrand, was *not* Bertrand.

### Kerry Thornley

Garrison obtained indictments against individuals who, like Andrews, failed to co-operate with him; to re-call Gurvich's words, he "put the screws on" these "potential witnesses" largely as a means of garnering publicity, since it became evident that the press seldom questioned the relevance of these peripheral indict-ments to the main case being prosecuted against Clay Shaw. And every successful indictment (if not convic-tion) on a charge of perjury at least *appeared* to en-hance the image of the District Attorney's success and the validity of his investigation. In fact, Garrison seemed, on occasion, less concerned with indicting key figures in the investigation than with obtaining indictments *per se*—even if this involved turning friendly witnesses into suspects. The case of Kerry Thornley is particularly enlightening in this regard.

In October 1967, while Garrison was visiting Los Angeles to raise funds for his investigation, he met with David Lifton, a man who had spent considerable time doing independent research into the Kennedy assassination. According to Lifton,[22] Garrison solicited his help in obtaining the "co-operation" of Kerry Thornley, a friend of Lifton's who had served with Lee Harvey Oswald in the Marine Corps in 1959 and who, after the assassination, had written a brief book about Oswald. Garrison explained that Thornley was to play an essential role in his plan to indict for perjury one John R. Heindel, who had also served in the Marines with Oswald. Garrison said that he had reason to believe that Heindel was the man Thornley had once overheard speaking Russian with Oswald, and he wanted Thornley to confirm the fact publicly and under oath. The plan was quite simple: Garrison would first call Heindel before the grand jury and ask him to state whether or not he had ever heard Oswald speaking Russian; Heindel would, as he had previously stated, answer that he had not. Then Garrison would call Thornley before the grand jury and ask him to state whether he had ever heard Heindel speaking Russian with Oswald; Thornley would answer that he had, and Heindel would then be indicted for perjury. Although the question of whether or not Oswald had ever spoken Russian in the presence of Heindel was palpably irrelevant—to the investigations of both the Warren Commission and Garrison—the news stories that Heindel's arrest would produce could be, in Garrison's opinion, quite advantageous to his case. As he explained to Lifton, Heindel's nickname in the Marine Corps had been "Hidel," which was nearly the same as the alias, "A. J. Hidell," which Oswald had used several times, most notably to order the rifle he allegedly used in the assassination. Garrison told Lifton that he could already envision the splendid news stories that would develop out of Heindel's arrest: "John R. Heindel, alias 'Hidel,' was today arrested in New Orleans in the conspiracy investigation. . . ." And aside from the publicity the indictment would generate, Garrison indicated that he could use it as a "legal lever" to induce Heindel to give testimony relevant to his court case against Clay Shaw. "This could be the break I've been waiting for," he declared.[23]

Lifton finally agreed to discuss the matter with Thornley. After Garrison returned to New Orleans, however, Lifton did some investigating of his own, determined that Heindel was probably not the person with whom Oswald had reportedly been conversing in Russian, and immediately telegraphed that information to Garrison. Although Heindel could not be arrested without the "co-operation" of Lifton and Thornley, which would not now be forthcoming, Garrison realized that he could still create the sort of conflict of testimony he had originally intended to use in indicting Heindel—simply by using it with reference to a different candidate for perjury: Kerry Thornley.

Several weeks after their first meeting, Lifton and Garrison had another discussion in Los Angeles regarding Thornley. Lifton's account of the meeting runs as follows:

> We sat down in chairs. Garrison then fixed me with this "mystical stare" of his, and said, in a slow, even tone, as if making some type of biblical pronouncement: "Thornley lied." (He stretched out the word "lied," by pausing on the *i* sound for about a second or two.)
>
> This took me quite by surprise. After all, only three weeks ago Thornley was to be Garrison's star witness-to-be.
>
> Why, I asked, did he say Thornley lied?

Pause.

Again, "Thornley lied." (As if, by repeating it, it gained in validity.)

Then Garrison told me: "Thornley lied when he said he didn't know Oswald in September 1963." Again, I was dumbfounded. I politely offered the thought that I would go wherever the evidence led; what evidence did he have that this was the case?

Then, Garrison told me: "We have so many witnesses who saw them together at that time we have stopped looking for more."

Then, another pontifical pronouncement: "Thornley's with the CIA."

"But why do you say that, Jim?" I asked.

"Thornley worked at a hotel in Arlington, Virginia."

So what, I wanted to know. My "so what?" type of rebuttal was met by his incredulity, as if "What do you mean, 'so what?'; isn't it obvious to you what this means?"[24]

Garrison also told Lifton that although Thornley denied he had seen Oswald in New Orleans in 1963, his office had located another witness who claimed to have seen Oswald and Thornley dining together in a New Orleans restaurant that year. The witness turned out to be Barbara Reed, a French Quarter resident who reputedly practices voodoo and has from time to time assisted Garrison's investigators by "screening witnesses."[25]

Garrison proceeded to subpoena Thornley before the grand jury. His testimony to the effect that he had not seen Oswald in New Orleans in 1963 did in fact conflict with the sworn testimony of Barbara Reed, and Thornley was subsequently indicted for perjury.* Thus, as Lifton notes, Garrison succeeded in doing to Thornley precisely what he had originally hoped to do to John Heindel with Thornley's aid.

What is really outrageous is that Kerry's subpoena to come to New Orleans to testify was not issued by a man who sought to find out facts, or find out truth, but to *do to Kerry exactly and precisely* what Garrison had intended doing to Heindel!

In other words, Garrison had a theory about Heindel, a theory which posited Heindel's involvement in the assassination, at least after the fact. The point is, Garrison thought Heindel "knew something" and was "hiding" it.

The method for "breaking" Heindel was to get Heindel to testify, get Thornley to testify, establishing a conflict of testimony. Then Heindel was to be charged with perjury, with Kerry (and others) presumably being the witnesses against Heindel.

---

* Apparently Garrison had entertained other plans regarding Thornley. At one time, it was thought he might serve as a likely "second Oswald" —that is, the individual who, according to Professor Richard Popkin's theory, impersonated Oswald before the assassination as part of a ruse for foiling the investigators. In what was evidently an effort to help Garrison realize this plan, Harold Weisberg, whose series of books critical of the Warren Report includes the one entitled *Photographic Whitewash*, sent a letter on the District Attorney's office stationery to Fred Newcomb, a photographer in California, saying, "Enclosed are four sets of pictures of Kerry Thornley printed backwards but otherwise the resemblance to Oswald and his receding hairline, which when his hair is combed the opposite of his normal fashion, is quite emphatic. What I would like you to do with one of each pair is pretend you were a make-up man doing the minimum necessary to make Thornley look as much as possible like Oswald as for example by pruning off or brushing back the forelock, trimming the eyebrows, shadowing the chin, etc. I would like you to keep one pair for your use out there, send one pair to me and the other two to Jim Garrison. . . ."[26]

Now, Garrison called Kerry to New Orleans to do
the same thing to him.[27]

Thornley's indictment was the twelfth ancillary case
arising out of Garrison's main investigation into the
conspiracy charges against Clay Shaw. Six of these
involved unco-operative witnesses—Kerry Thornley
(perjury), Dean Andrews (perjury), Layton Martens,
an acquaintance of Ferrie's (perjury), John Cancler (contempt of court), Sergio Arcacha Smith (burglary), and Morris Brownlee (possession of narcotics);
three involved newsmen who had been critical of Garrison—David Chandler (perjury), Walter Sheridan of
NBC (public bribery), and Richard Townley of
WDSU-TV (intimidation of a witness); two involved
former members of Garrison's own staff—Gordon Novel
(burglary) and William Gurvich (petit larceny); and
one involved a man who, at least according to Dean
Andrews, doesn't even exist—Manuel Garcia Gonzales
(narcotics). Add to this list the several other newsmen, FBI agents, two directors of the CIA (Allen
Dulles and Richard Helms), two administrators of
the National Archives in Washington, D.C., Cuban
exile leaders, and various other persons subpoenaed
to appear before the Orleans Parish Grand Jury, and
it becomes clear that the District Attorney exercised
his considerable powers not simply to harass unco-
operative witnesses but to create as well the impression that certain important individuals were somehow
involved in the conspiracy under investigation.

# 2

# The Second Conspiracy

# VI

---

# The Tangled Web

The very repetition of a charge lends it a certain credibility, since people have a tendency to believe that where there's smoke there's fire.

—Jim Garrison in *Playboy* (discussing charges against him)

The principal consideration operating to restrain a duly elected district attorney from making indiscriminate arrests and charges—aside from normal ethical considerations—is fear of exposure by the press if supporting proof should not be forthcoming. Yet, despite some cogent evidence of malfeasance on Garrison's part reported by a number of journalists, public-opinion polls indicated that there was actually a substantial increase in the number of people, not only in Louisiana but throughout the country, who shared Garrison's belief in a conspiracy. If in fact his case was based on little more than wild rumors and the unsubstantiated testimony of unstable witnesses, why was the press so ineffective in checking Garrison? In his study of the late Senator Joseph R. McCarthy, Richard H. Rovere demonstrates how a certain kind of demagogue, when he is assailed by the press, can turn the hostile criticism to his own advantage. Such a demagogue builds his political base on the systematic exploitation of inchoate fears, and sets about organizing a popular flight from reality. To him, even the most vocal censure, however adverse its ostensible effect, represents useful publicity, for the more rigorously he is assaulted by the press, the more prominently he figures in the popular imagination. A false charge has to be repeated if it is to be refuted, and if the charge happens to be more appealing than the truth, it is entirely possible that it, rather than its refutation, will win general credence. This is especially likely to occur if the demagogue's charge offers a more or less plausible explanation of disturbing events, and if its refutation depends on the word of government officials, since the people most apt to accept conspiratorial interpretations of history are those who are most suspicious of both complexity and authority. As Rovere points out with regard to McCarthy, the demagogue soon learns that "the penalties for a really audacious mendacity are not as severe as the average politician fears them to be, that, in fact, there may be no penalties at all, but only profit."[1]

In a sense, the man who exploits popular fears builds his reputation on the prestige of his adversaries. The more impressive the list of detractors he can cite, the more important his charges appear to be. "Why are they trying to destroy me?" the demagogue asks. But the surest benefits he derives from being publicly criti-

cized are the "right to reply"—a right that is greatly
enhanced by the demands of day-to-day reporting,
which cause the press to focus more directly on the
individual under attack than on the general issue at
stake—and the results of the ethic of "objective reporting"—which usually in practice means no more than
that the individual criticized gets the last word in the
news stories. If the demagogue is challenged on radio
or television, he can demand equal time to respond.
And, of course, his reply need not restrict itself to a
defense of his original position. Indeed, to obfuscate
the issue further and mitigate the attack on him, the
demagogue may strike out in an altogether different
direction. For he is, typically, concerned not with
substantive issues but with ways of manipulating the
emotions of the electorate.

One way Garrison responded to attacks made on
his thesis that there was a conspiracy to kill President
Kennedy was by talking about a second conspiracy
that grew out of the first one—a conspiracy of secrecy
dedicated to concealing the truth about the assassination. As in a speech he gave in December 1967 in
New Mexico, entitled "The Rise of the Fourth Reich,
or How to Conceal the Truth about an Assassination without Really Trying," Garrison often seemed
more deeply preoccupied with exposing an insidious
misprision of felony on the part of federal authorities than with establishing the facts of the assassination itself.[2] To be sure, such an obsessional concern
with governmental suppression is not a new phenomenon, nor is it limited to the assassination issue.
The political-sociologist Edward Shils has pointed to a

highly suggestive link between the generalized fear of secrecy and the Populist tradition in America. In his book *The Torment of Secrecy*, he argues that a repugnance toward secrecy is so deeply ingrained in American political life that even in matters involving national security, secrecy is tolerated only as a necessary evil.[3] To exploit this fear of secrecy, a truly Machiavellian politician could be expected to portray himself as engaged in a life-and-death struggle to wrest secrets from some powerful elite that controls the government and the news media, and to interpret all criticism leveled against him as part of a plot to conceal the dark truth from the populace.

### Attack and Counterattack: The *Saturday Evening Post*

The first full-scale criticism of Garrison came in the last week of April 1967, in the *Saturday Evening Post*, when, in his article entitled "Rush to Judgment in New Orleans," James Phelan revealed that the crucial part of Perry Raymond Russo's testimony—the section incriminating Clay Shaw—was contradicted by a statement Russo had made earlier to Assistant District Attorney Sciambra.[4] The day Phelan's story appeared, a bold headline in the *New Orleans States-Item* announced, "MOUNTING EVIDENCE LINKS CIA TO 'PLOT' PROBE." The article under this head, which implied that the CIA was attempting to block Garrison's efforts, because former agents were involved in the conspiracy, had been prepared by several *States-Item* reporters, including Hoke May and Ross Yockey, who reportedly had a close working relationship with the Garrison investigation.[5] Whether by design or by accident, the charges against the CIA effectively overshadowed the Phelan story, at least in New Orleans.

### Newsweek and the CIA

Two weeks later, in an article written by Hugh Aynesworth, Newsweek reported that a friend of David Ferrie's had been offered a three-thousand-dollar bribe to implicate Clay Shaw in the conspiracy. The offer had been secretly tape-recorded by the witness's lawyer. Although the tape left it unclear whether the money was to be in payment for true information or false, it was damaging under any circumstances. (At one point, Garrison's representative said, "We can change the story around.")[6] When Garrison learned of the impending Newsweek disclosure, he prepared a memorandum on CIA participation in the assassination; this document promptly found its way into the hands of Yockey and May, who wrote it up in an exclusive story in the States-Item.[7] Upon being asked about the Newsweek charges, Garrison answered by confirming the States-Item report on the CIA. "The federal agents who concealed vital knowledge regarding President Kennedy's assassination, and their superiors who are now engaged in a dedicated effort to discredit and obstruct the gathering of evidence, are guilty of being accessories after the fact to one of the cruelest murders in our history," he declared, and he went on to warn that "the arrogant totalitarian efforts of these federal agencies to obstruct the discovery of truth is a matter which I intend to bring to light."[8] An article in the *New York Times* the following day attested to Garrison's success in blurring these charges with his own: although the *Times* article focused on the *Newsweek* report, the headline read, "GARRISON CHARGES CIA AND FBI CONCEAL EVIDENCE ON OSWALD."[9]

Garrison continued his offensive by issuing a subpoena for Richard Helms, the director of the Central Intelligence Agency, demanding that Helms produce a photograph showing Oswald in the company of a CIA agent in Mexico.[10] Subsequently, it was made plain that Garrison had no reason to believe that a photograph showing Oswald with a CIA agent had ever existed,[11] but Garrison's subpoena drew national coverage and tended to dilute further the effect of the *Newsweek* story. It is worth noting that before Garrison subpoenaed the director of the CIA he had considered another move—arresting Regis Kennedy, an FBI agent in New Orleans who had taken part in the government's investigation of the assassination. Garrison explained to William Gurvich that although the agent would deny the charge, the denial would only add to the effect of criminally charging an FBI agent. But Garrison had second thoughts about attacking the FBI and, according to Gurvich, chose the CIA because, as Garrison himself put it, "they can't afford to answer."[12]

Later, in May, when his claim that the notation of a Dallas post-office box in Clay Shaw's address book was actually Ruby's encoded telephone number was debunked by Lee Odom, the owner of the box, Garrison, it will be recalled, countered by charging that Oswald's address book contained an encoded version of the local CIA telephone number in New Orleans (though he later had to admit that the code was "subjective"). Then, further obscuring questions arising from his dubious interpretation of the "telephone codes," Garrison stated that both Oswald and Ruby had been CIA agents, and asserted on a local television show a few days later that the CIA knew the identity of the other assassins but, he said, "we can't find out [their names] with the CIA keeping its vaults locked."[13]

## NBC and "Thought Control"

On the evening of June 19, 1967, NBC devoted an hour to a critical examination of Garrison's investigation, entitled "The JFK Conspiracy: The Case of Jim Garrison." The first part of the program dealt with Russo's allegation that he had seen Oswald, Shaw, and Ferrie plotting the assassination at a party in Ferrie's apartment in September 1963. The NBC reporters demonstrated that at least one other person present at the party had not seen Shaw or Oswald there, and that Ferrie's bearded roommate, who Russo claimed was Oswald, had been identified by other people at the party as James Lewallen. The program then concentrated on Garrison's investigative methods, and a parade of witnesses was presented to allege that Garrison representatives had attempted to bribe or intimidate them. In addition, NBC revealed that both of Garrison's key witnesses, Russo and Vernon Bundy, had failed lie-detector tests before testifying at the preliminary hearing. Frank McGee, the NBC anchor man, concluded, "The case he has built against Clay Shaw is based on testimony that did not pass a lie-detector test Garrison ordered—and Garrison knew it."[14] The lie-detector evidence that NBC used to cap its case against Garrison was almost certainly the weakest part of that case. Yet the fact that NBC found it necessary to conclude its program with a concise statement of evidence established by the familiar and easily understood lie detector suggests a problem the mass media, and especially television, have in demonstrating a complex truth to their audience. Although the lie detector carries a certain authority in the popular imagination, and appears to give an unambiguous answer—the man is either lying or telling the truth—it is in fact merely a device for measuring the emotional stress that a witness is undergoing while he is being questioned. Such stress may indicate nervousness over deception, or it may indicate any of a number of other emotional responses. Since there is no objective way of differentiating among these responses, FBI director J. Edgar Hoover had advised the Warren Commission in a memorandum that lie-detector tests were unreliable and of dubious value.[15] NBC had assembled a good deal of cogent, if complex, evidence to show that Russo's allegation was untrue. But the effort to resolve, for its mass audience, the difficult issue it had so painstakingly presented by resorting to a simple and readily comprehensible indictment based on evidence drawn from a source as dubious as lie-detector tests left the program's conclusions open to serious criticism.*

Garrison, however, did not bother with serious criticism of the program's content; instead, he launched his counterattack by denouncing NBC as a party to an "Establishment" conspiracy to destroy him. "All of the screaming and hollering now being heard is evidence that we have caught a very large fish," he proclaimed the morning after the NBC show. "It is obvious that there are elements in Washington, D.C., which are desperate because we are in the process of uncovering their hoax."[16] To account for NBC's interest in his investigation, he told an interviewer that the network "is owned by Radio Corporation of America, one of the top ten defense contractors in the country." (It is actually twenty-seventh, according to the Department of Defense.) Garrison added, "All of these ladies of the evening are very much alike—the preferred customer is the one with the big bankroll and any position he suggests is eagerly assumed." Moreover, Garrison implied that the program had been secretly financed by the CIA.[17]

Garrison wrote to the Federal Communications Commission to demand equal time, and NBC granted him a half hour of prime evening time on July 15, 1967, to reply to the charges. Once on the air, however, he said, "I am not even going to bother to dignify the foolishness which Newsweek and NBC and some of the other news agencies have tried to make you believe

---

* NBC was not alone in employing lie detectors. Newsweek, the Chicago Tribune, and the Hearst Headline Service also used them to demonstrate that Garrison's case was based on untruths.

about my office," and went on to denounce the media for manipulating the news and practicing "thought control." After giving five specific examples of "suppressed news," he presented his familiar argument that the attacks on his case attested to its validity: ". . . if our investigation was as haywire as they would like to have you think, then you would not see such a coordinated barrage coming from the news centers in the East." And he concluded, ". . . as long as I am alive, no one is going to stop me from seeing that you obtain the full truth, and nothing less than the full truth, and no fairy tales."[18] Garrison had an audience of some twenty million, and for that, he said in his *Playboy* interview, he was "singularly grateful to Walter Sheridan," one of those who had prepared the NBC critique of his case.[19]

Garrison's gratitude was less than total. Not long after the NBC program, he issued warrants for the arrest of Sheridan and also Richard Townley, who had assisted in the preparation of the show, charging them with attempted bribery. Specifically, Garrison alleged that they had offered Perry Russo a free trip to California.[20]* But if this offer technically constituted an act of bribery, Garrison himself had taken considerable pains to bait the trap. He told me himself that he had directed Russo to speak to the reporters over a monitored phone and inquire what protection they could offer him if he were to change his testimony. The purpose was, as he put it, "to give NBC enough rope to

---

* Both Sheridan and Townley unequivocally denied the charges. Sheridan told me that it was Russo himself who suggested that NBC pay his expenses to California.

hang itself." In his public statement on the matter, Garrison charged that the NBC program "will probably stand for many years to come as a symbol of the length to which some powerful outside interests are willing to go in order to interfere with state government." The cases are still pending.[21]

## CBS and the "Establishment"

Shortly after Garrison's skirmish with NBC, William Gurvich resigned as one of his chief investigators, after telling the late Senator Robert F. Kennedy that there was no basis in fact and no material evidence in Garrison's case.[22] Gurvich then appeared on the CBS-TV "News Inquiry" into the assassination and said he had resigned because "I saw no reason for the investigation. . . . The truth, as I see it, is that Mr. Shaw should never have been arrested."[23] Gurvich's private-detective agency had conducted most of the lie-detector tests that Garrison had ordered, and at the time of his resignation Gurvich had in his possession a master file of the principal evidence in the case. This defection not only made for embarrassing headlines but opened up the possibility that Garrison's fund of confidential information—or his lack of such a fund—would be made public. In a statement to the press, Garrison described Gurvich's resignation as "the latest move from the Eastern headquarters of the Establishment to attempt to discredit our investigation." It was all part of a coordinated plot against him.[24] In another press release, he said, "All they are doing is proving two things: first, that we were correct when we uncovered the involvement of the Central Intelligence Agency in the assassination; second, that there is something very wrong today with our government in Washington, D.C., inasmuch as it is willing to use massive economic power to conceal the truth from the people."[25] Later, in his *Playboy* interview, Garrison implied that Gurvich had been a CIA infiltrator from the start.[26] He also charged Gurvich with petty larceny, claiming the file that he had was worth nineteen dollars. And, for good measure, he charged on the ABC "Page One" television show that Senator Robert Kennedy whom Gurvich had earlier been in touch with, was "without any question of a doubt . . . interfering with the investigation of the murder of his brother" and was making "a real effort to stop it."[27]

### Pseudo-Attacks: Earl Warren and Lyndon B. Johnson

After it had become quite clear that criticism of Garrison's case could be used to generate a specter of conspiracy, Garrison took the logical next step and started creating pseudo-attacks on himself. When reporters in Tokyo asked Chief Justice Earl Warren his opinion of the Garrison investigation, he replied, "I want to skirt this very carefully, because the case could someday come before the Supreme Court." Pressed as to whether Garrison possessed any evidence that might contradict the findings of the Commission he had headed, the Chief Justice answered, "I've heard that he claims to have such information, but I haven't seen any."[28] Garrison immediately characterized this "new counterattack" as "heavy artillery whistling in from

Tokyo," and said in a press release, "It is a little disconcerting to find the Chief Justice of the United States on his hands and knees trying to tie some sticks of dynamite to the case. However, the Chief Justice is a practical man and I expect he knows what he is doing. . . . The last time he was called into action to perform a service was when the President of the United States was assassinated by men who had been connected with the Central Intelligence Agency."[29] Garrison predicted a new broadside from the federal authorities: "Judging from the careful co-ordination which the Establishment showed in its last offensive against the case, it is safe to expect that other elements of the federal government and national press will now follow up with a new effort to discredit the case and the prosecution."[30]

Another example of Garrison's technique involved Gordon Novel, the electronics expert, who had told him about Ferrie's participation in a "pickup" of munitions from the Schlumberger Well Surveying company, in Houma, Louisiana. Novel rapidly advanced from advising Garrison on anti-eavesdropping techniques, the business that had first brought him to Garrison's attention, to become a witness against Ferrie and, at least in Garrison's mind, an "investigator." Then, according to one account, Garrison was told that his investigator had been furnishing information to NBC reporters, and Novel was subpoenaed to appear before a grand jury.[31] Instead of appearing, Novel left the state and went to Ohio. Garrison filed burglary charges against Novel, alleging that he had participated in the conspiracy to steal arms from the Schlumberger company, and he was arrested in Ohio.[32] After some initial reluctance, Ohio Governor James Rhodes finally agreed to extradite Novel to Louisiana if Garrison would complete the papers within sixty days.[33] Garrison, however, did not take the necessary steps. As the deadline approached, Assistant District Attorney Alcock asked if he should return the papers to Ohio, and Garrison told him not to bother.[34] After Garrison failed to reply to phone calls and telegrams from Ohio authorities inquiring about his intentions in the Novel case, and after the sixty-day period had elapsed, Judge William T. Gillie dismissed the extradition case against Novel.[35] And yet in the *Playboy* interview, Garrison insisted, "The reason we were unable to obtain Novel's extradition from Ohio . . . is that there are powerful forces in Washington who find it imperative to conceal from the American public the truth about the assassination."[36] He went on to indicate that Novel was now a material witness in his case and, according to attorneys for Novel, implied that his former "investigator" was somehow connected with the conspiracy. (Novel filed suit against Garrison and *Playboy* for ten million dollars in punitive and compensatory damages.) And in a speech to the Radio and Television News Association of Southern California, in Los Angeles, Garrison cited his failure to obtain Novel's extradition as evidence that President Johnson was putting pressure on local officials to secrete witnesses from him. He went on to accuse President Johnson of preventing "the people in this country from seeing the evidence," and asserted, with the logic of *cui bono*, ". . . the fact that he has profited from the assassination most, more than any other man, makes it imperative that he see that the evidence is released, so that we can know that he is not involved. . . ."[37]

## The New Yorker

When part of this book was first published in The New Yorker in July 1968, Garrison responded in his customary style. Calling a press conference, the District Attorney announced that an "intelligence agency of a foreign country . . . successfully penetrated the assassination operation," and that the "detailed information" he had received from this unnamed intelligence agency had "corroborated" statements he had previously made that President Kennedy was assassinated "by elements of the Central Intelligence Agency."[38] He frankly admitted, according to Time, that the timing of the disclosure of the foreign assassination study was "designed to rebut" the charges in the New Yorker article[39] (which he said was part of a "CIA-inspired campaign" to discredit his investigation).[40] The "intelligence study" that Garrison referred to turned out to be nothing more than a pseudonymous manuscript entitled "The Plot" that had been sent to him three months earlier, after the New York Review of Books had rejected it. According to Bethell, Garrison deduced that the manuscript "must have been written by a foreign intelligence agency, and probably the KGB" (the Russian counterpart of the CIA) because it contained "inside information" about the assassination. Actually, a good deal of the "inside information" that Garrison referred to had been, I found, previously published in William Manchester's *Death of a President* and in Garrison's own *Playboy* interview. Garrison referred the manuscript to *Ramparts*, whose editor also decided not to publish it, after it was learned that the author was merely a dissident European writer and not a "foreign intelligence agency." Yet Garrison's deployment of this manuscript was at least tactically effective: the headlines of the *New Orleans Times-Picayune* on July 12, the day *The New Yorker* appeared in New Orleans, read: "FOREIGN GROUP HAS FACTS—D.A., CIA ROLE IN JFK DEATH CONFIRMED, HE SAYS."[41]

# VII

# The CIA

If the director of the CIA and the top officials of
the CIA were in the jurisdiction of Louisiana, I
would charge them without hesitation.

—Jim Garrison, May 21, WWL-TV,
New Orleans

Garrison's technique in expounding the so-called second conspiracy is typical of what Richard Hofstadter
has classified as "the paranoid style in American politics," to which "the feeling of persecution is central,"
and which is "systematized in grandiose theories of conspiracy."[1] Still, the fact that Garrison expressed his
ideas in a paranoid style does not of itself rule out
the possibility that there is substance to his claims.
Is the CIA, for example, really concealing some involvement of its agents in the assassination, as Garrison has claimed? In May 1967, Garrison declared on
the ABC "Issues and Answers" television program,
"Of course the Central Intelligence Agency had no
role in the planning or intending the assassination

of President Kennedy. I think that would be a ridiculous position for anyone to take."[2] He has, however, taken precisely that position on several occasions. His allegations regarding the culpability of the CIA have varied widely. On May 9, 1967, the CIA was accused of merely concealing evidence;[3] by May 18, Oswald and Ruby were themselves identified by Garrison as CIA employees;[4] on May 21, the District Attorney stated that the CIA knew "the name of every man involved and the name of the individuals who pulled the triggers";[5] on May 24, he added that the CIA was presently hiding the killers' whereabouts;[6] on November 14, he decided that "employees—a limited number —of the Central Intelligence Agency of the U.S. government are involved in the assassination";[7] on January 31, 1968, he said on the Johnny Carson show that "the Central Intelligence Agency was deeply involved in the assassination";[8] and in February he said in an interview filmed for Dutch television that "President Kennedy was killed by elements of the Central Intelligence Agency of the United States government," going on to explain, "The Central Intelligence Agency . . . had worked for a long time creating the tableau— the cover scene—beforehand. This is standard for a Central Intelligence Agency assassination. As a matter of fact, the CIA, when it conducts an assassination, describes it as an executive action. This takes the sin out of it. As a matter of fact, to the CIA employees, the sin then becomes failing to do your job properly, in the executive action. Of course, even as I describe it, I'm conscious of the parallels with regard to Germany under Hitler. What I'm talking about is nothing less than Fascism, which has arrived in America. . . ."[9]

Just how solid the basis for these charges is can be deduced from Garrison's twenty-six-page interview in *Playboy*, which is doubtless the fullest and most coherent single presentation of his case to date. When he was pressed by *Playboy's* interviewer, Eric Norden, for the evidence on which his charges of CIA complicity were based, Garrison mentioned eight specific items: (1) a missing CIA photograph that shows Oswald in the company of a CIA agent in Mexico before the assassination, (2) classified files on David Ferrie, which "would indicate the existence of a conspiracy involving former employees of the CIA to kill the President," (3) suppressed autopsy X-rays and photographs of President Kennedy's body and "other vital evidence," which also reveal that former CIA agents took part in the murder, (4) CIA files that reveal, it is implied, that Oswald was involved in the CIA's U-2 project, (5) the fact that the CIA destroyed a document that the Warren Commission had requested, (6) the identification of Oswald's CIA "babysitter," (7) the identification of a CIA "courier," and (8) "the consistent refusal of the federal government" to provide Garrison with "any information" about the role of the CIA in the assassination. This last piece of "evidence" Garrison calls "the clincher."[10]

At least half of the "evidence" on which Garrison's repertory of charges against the CIA was based is itself deduced from evidence that Garrison had never seen. He accomplished this trick by simply sketching in on the *tabula rasa* of missing (or nonexistent) evidence facts that appear to incriminate the CIA. If the evidence is missing, a revelation of its contents is not, of course, easily refuted. And the old suspicion of secrecy qua secrecy also plays a part. "If there's nothing to hide," people wonder, "why is the thing missing in the first place?" Consider Item 1, the missing CIA photographs, on which Garrison based his original charge that the CIA was concealing vital evidence.

## 1. The Missing Photograph

When Garrison subpoenaed Richard Helms, the director of the CIA, he instructed him to produce a photograph that CIA agents had taken in Mexico City about seven weeks before the assassination and that, Garrison claimed, showed Oswald in front of the Cuban Embassy in the company of a CIA agent.[11] The supposed facts conveyed by this missing snapshot were what led Garrison to assert that the CIA knew the identity of Kennedy's assassins and was concealing the truth. But how had this information been deduced from a missing photograph, which Garrison admitted that he had never seen?

Actually, the story of the CIA photograph had its origin in an incident I myself first reported, in my book *Inquest*, as a means of illustrating the problems that the Warren Commission lawyers faced in communicating with the CIA. According to my account, a man in front of the Cuban Embassy in Mexico City had been routinely photographed before the assassina-

tion by a hidden CIA camera and identified as Lee
Harvey Oswald; the information had subsequently
been forwarded to the FBI. However, as it turned
out, I continued, the man in the photograph (which
was published in Volume XX of the Warren Commission's testimony and evidence) was obviously not Oswald but a heavy-set individual who could not be
identified. The staff lawyer Wesley J. Liebeler, who
was trying to clarify the incident for the Warren Commission, inquired of the CIA whether a photograph
showing Oswald in Mexico City did in fact exist. He
never received an answer.[12] Garrison postulated that
the CIA had forwarded the picture of a man who was
not Oswald and had withheld a photograph that *did*
show Oswald leaving the Cuban Embassy. Furthermore, he conjectured that the most likely reason for
suppressing such a photograph was that it revealed
Oswald to be in the company of another man—and
since the identity of this man was being concealed, he
must have been working for the CIA.[13] It seems unlikely that Garrison had any knowledge of this photograph other than what he gathered from the account
of it in my book, because he repeats the details of
that account, including a certain erroneous detail.
Liebeler, who originally told me the story, pointed
out a few weeks after *Inquest* was published that the
picture in question had been taken of a man in front
of the Soviet Embassy in Mexico City, not the Cuban
Embassy. Yet Garrison repeated the erroneous information (my own) to contrive an ominous piece of
"evidence" that was not simply "missing" but nonexistent.

## 2. The Missing Ferrie Files

Garrison relied on a similar device in his second item of "evidence," asserting that files on Ferrie were classified because they "would indicate the existence of a conspiracy involving former employees of the CIA."[14] The files Garrison referred to consist of FBI reports on the activities and private life of David Ferrie. After the assassination, FBI agents interviewed a number of Ferrie's associates and turned these reports over to the Warren Commission, which then consigned them to the National Archives. A good portion of these was made public, while the remainder, about thirty-six pages, was kept classified on the grounds that it contained information that might be damaging to innocent parties.[15] (Wesley Liebeler, who also conducted this part of the investigation, told me that these files mainly concerned Ferrie's circle of homosexual acquaintances.)[16] Exactly how Garrison could specify what would be indicated by FBI reports he had never seen is problematical, but again the *tabula rasa* of missing evidence gives him an opportunity to sketch in unverifiable details of a CIA conspiracy.

## 3. The Missing X-rays, Photos, Film Frames

In his third "proof" of CIA complicity, Garrison states that "the President's autopsy X-rays and photos and other vital evidence in this case are classified because they would indicate the existence of a conspiracy, involving former employees of the CIA, to kill the President."[17] And in a subsequent statement, he charged more specifically that "Lyndon Johnson's administration is still keeping it [the autopsy material] secret."[18] While it is true that the X-ray and autopsy photographs were never examined by the Warren Commission—and it is certainly possible, as I pointed out in *Inquest*, that a proper examination of this basic evidence could undermine (or, on the other hand, confirm) the Commission's conclusions about the autopsy—it does not necessarily follow that this material has been classified by the Johnson administration, as Garrison suggests, to protect the CIA. In fact, the material was "classified" not by the government but by the Kennedy family, which came in possession of it after the autopsy examination, and subsequently, in 1966, deposited it in the National Archives on the condition that it not be opened to examination to private citizens for a period of five years and thereafter only to persons professionally qualified to evaluate medical evidence. To be sure, the very fact that it was unavailable provided Garrison with "secret evidence": he could claim in his public statements—without fear of immediate refutation—that the CIA was implicated in the conspiracy.

Every once in a while, the evidence proved to exist, and Garrison was caught in the act. For example, he stated in his *Playboy* interview that four frames of the famous Abraham Zapruder film of the assassination—numbers 208-211—were missing from the frame-by-frame reproduction of the film in the testimony and evidence published by the Warren Commission, and he went on to claim that these frames "reveal signs of stress appearing suddenly on the back of a street sign" and to suggest that "these signs of stress may very well have been caused by the impact of a stray bullet on the sign."[19] But frames 208-211, while missing from the Warren volumes, are not missing from a copy of the film that *Life* holds; and after Garrison's charges in *Playboy* were published, George P. Hunt, the managing editor of *Life*, announced that the magazine was releasing for publication frames 207-212 of the Zapruder film—which included the ones Garrison had alleged were missing—for the purpose of ending "what has become an irrelevant discussion." What Garrison termed "the missing frames" have in fact been published in Josiah Thompson's book *Six Seconds in Dallas*, and they reveal no "signs of stress."[20]

## 4. The National Archives

In his fourth item, Garrison supposedly reveals the contents of classified CIA documents in the National Archives. These documents were prepared for the Warren Commission by the CIA. And although the title of each of these reports—usually referring to the general topic on which Commission lawyers requested that the CIA provide information or answer queries—is listed in the index of Commission documents, the reports themselves are classified, as are all CIA reports containing the names of operatives, informers, and foreign sources. Garrison customarily rattles off the titles of the "suppressed CIA files," as he calls them, and then sets forth their "contents" in his own terms. For example, in *Playboy* he cited Commission Document No. 931, entitled "Oswald's Access to Information About the U-2," and then ominously suggested that Oswald was involved in the U-2 program.[21] He amplified on this "evidence" in a speech he made after the *Playboy* interview appeared, stating, "The reason you can't see that [Commission Document No. 931] for many years is because you will then realize that Lee Oswald was then working for the United States government, as a CIA employee, and they don't want you to know that."[22] Garrison "used" this classified document, which, of course, he had not seen, to substantiate the charge that Oswald acted as a CIA agent. Yet testimony in the Warren Report indicates that it may well contain information on what Oswald heard when, during his stay in the Soviet Union, he dropped in on the trial of the U-2 pilot Francis Gary Powers. In any event, it seems highly unlikely that if the CIA were indeed as sinister as Garrison alleges, it would *admit* in a report to the Commission that Oswald was a CIA agent, especially since its reports were to be read by lawyers working for the Commission who were not (as my own interviews with them demonstrate) particularly inclined to be secretive.

### 5. The Secret CIA Memo

Garrison asserted that the Warren Commission was never able to obtain "a secret CIA memo on Oswald's activities in Russia"—a memo attached to a State Department document—because the memorandum had been "destroyed" the day after the assassination. This statement is simply untrue. While it is true that one copy of this memorandum was destroyed while being photocopied, another copy was duly forwarded to the Commission on May 8, 1964, as is evident from Volume XVIII of the Commission's testimony and evidence.[23] When Sylvia Meagher, who has indexed the twenty-six volumes of the Warren Commission testimony and evidence—and has tried earnestly to correct the mistakes of the critics as well as those of the Commission—pointed out to Garrison that his charge was based on a fallacy, he acknowledged the error; even so, he went on using the non-fact to support his charge that the CIA was "incinerating" evidence.[24]

### 6. The CIA "Babysitter"

The sixth item of evidence, the identity of Oswald's CIA "babysitter," was extrapolated from a purchase order for ten Ford trucks.[25] Oscar Deslatte, the assistant manager of a New Orleans Ford agency, who wrote up the order on January 20, 1961, subsequently reported to the FBI that his customers told him the trucks were to be used by an organization known as "Friends of Democratic Cuba" and requested a discount. Deslatte listed the purchaser of the trucks as "Oswald" (no first name given) and said that the individual with "Oswald" called himself Joseph Moore. When FBI agents asked Deslatte about the incident, he said that he could "neither describe nor identify either of the men."[26] Garrison believes, however, that the purchase was made for the CIA and that Moore, who has never been located, was in fact Oswald's CIA chaperon.[27] It is possible, of course, that Moore was the CIA "babysitter" of some Oswald, but in 1961, at the time the purchase order was filled out, Lee Harvey Oswald was working at the Byelorussian Radio and Television Factory in Minsk.[28]

## 7. The CIA "Courier"

The seventh item of evidence, concerning a CIA "courier," refers to Donald Philetus Norton, the convicted bank embezzler and night-club entertainer who, as mentioned earlier, had been thoroughly discredited as a witness and was jettisoned by Garrison himself even before he gave the *Playboy* interview.[29]

## 8. The "Clincher"

Garrison's "clincher," the assertion that the government had not revealed to him any information of the CIA's complicity in the assassination,[30] is a perfect example of Garrison's own brand of logic, in which the fact that he had not found or been given any evidence of CIA complicity was itself proof that the CIA was withholding evidence of its guilt.

Garrison also charged that the CIA was interfering with his investigation, citing as evidence the monitoring of his telephones and asserting that the CIA had paid for a Washington, D.C., trip for Ferrie's heir, Alvin Beauboeuf, and his lawyer and that "most of the attorneys for the hostile witnesses and defendants

were hired by the CIA."[31] This is hardly more substantial than the evidence he used to support his
charge of CIA complicity in the assassination. Garrison himself had earlier identified the FBI as the party
monitoring his telephones, and was so certain of this
that he had planned the midnight raid on the FBI's
New Orleans office in order to obtain the tapes of
monitored conversations. It was NBC, not the CIA,
which paid Beauboeuf's expenses to Washington in
conjunction with the program it was preparing on the
Garrison investigation.[32] Finally, the statement that
defendants' attorneys "were hired by the CIA"—a
charge the lawyers heatedly deny—reveals a curious
impatience with due process. Implicit in the District
Attorney's charge is the notion that the defendant's
right to counsel (no matter who pays for it) can be
construed as interference.

# VIII

# The Media

The press has now reached the point of subsequent control by the Central Intelligence Agency that we literally can't get the truth out.

—Jim Garrison, February 1968, on Dutch television

Although Garrison was given the opportunity to present his case on all three national television networks, and appeared on more television and radio programs than perhaps any other practicing district attorney in history, one of his major themes was that the press furtively controlled the news as a means of suppressing known facts about the John Kennedy assassination. "Behind the façade of earnest inquiry into the assassination is a thought-control project in the best tradition of *1984*," he has written. "Because of their role in the Establishment and their failure to conduct an effective inquiry, major news agencies have a vested interest in maintaining public ignorance."[1] Most of what Garrison has had to say on this subject has been

vague philippics, but in his half-hour NBC rebuttal
he did give five specific examples of news suppression,
and they are worth examining in detail. Of "powerful
news agencies," Garrison alleged:

> [1] They do not tell you that Lee Harvey Oswald's
> fingerprints were not found on the gun which was sup-
> posed to have killed the President.
> [2] And they do not tell you that nitrate tests exoner-
> ated Lee Oswald from the actual shooting by showing
> that he had not fired a rifle that day.
> [3] And they do not tell you that it was virtually
> impossible for Oswald to have taken his fingerprints off
> the gun, hidden the gun and gone down four flights of
> stairs by the time he was seen on the second floor.
> [4] Above all they do not tell you of the overwhelm-
> ing eyewitness testimony that shots were coming from
> behind the stone wall on the grassy knoll. . . .
> [5] You have not been told that Lee Oswald was in
> the employ of U.S. intelligence agencies, but this was
> the case.[2]

It is true that the public had not been told any of
these things, except by Garrison, but there is a good
reason for that. All five of the charges are either false
or captious.


### 1. Fingerprints

Fingerprints were indeed found on the rifle "which
was supposed to have killed the President," but the
prints could not be positively identified. This was not
particularly surprising. Sebastian F. Latona, a nationally
recognized fingerprint expert, testified before the War-

ren Commission that because of the unpolished finish of the rifle, which allowed it to absorb moisture, it was highly unlikely that an identifiable fingerprint would have been left on the weapon. Contrary to the popular impression regarding fingerprints, Latona noted, they are usually discernible only on highly polished surfaces.[3] What Garrison does not say is that a palmprint was discovered on the underside of the barrel of the rifle in question and that three different experts positively identified it as Oswald's.[4]*

## 2. The Nitrate Tests

Garrison's assertion that the nitrate tests "exonerated" Oswald is equally questionable. In the tests to which Garrison referred, the Dallas police made paraffin casts of Oswald's hands and right cheek, and these casts were then checked for traces of nitrates. Nitrates were found on the casts of both hands but not on the cast of his cheek. The test, however, in no way proves that Oswald did or did not fire a rifle. The nitrates found need not have come from gunpowder; many other substances—tobacco, matches, urine—will leave such residues. Conversely, the absence of nitrates indicates little, because a rifle (which, unlike a revolver, has no gap between the chamber and the barrel) is not as likely to leave nitrate traces on the cheek. In

---

* Although questions have been raised by critics about the circumstances under which this palmprint was found and removed on tape by Dallas police, laboratory tests conducted by the FBI indicate that the palmprint did indeed come from the rifle—since it bore impressions of the same irregularities that appeared on the barrel of the rifle.[5]

fact, the rifle in question was experimentally fired three times by an FBI agent, and no traces of nitrates were detected on his hands or cheek.[6] According to one FBI expert, Cortlandt Cunningham, the so-called paraffin test is completely unreliable, and its principal use in police work is simply to intimidate suspects; it produces more apprehension than valid evidence.[7] Garrison's suggestion that such tests could have proved that Oswald "had not fired a rifle that day" plays on the gullibility of the general public regarding the reliability of scientific-sounding data.

### 3. The Time Factor

As for Garrison's statement that it was "virtually impossible" for Oswald to have been on the second floor of the Book Depository building a few minutes after the assassination, it, too, is specious. A Secret Service agent, simulating Oswald's movements, reached the second floor from the sixth in one minute and eighteen seconds.[8] In any case, it is impossible to ascertain exactly what time Oswald was seen on the second floor; it could have been as long as five minutes after the assassination.

### 4. The Eyewitnesses

Garrison's next assertion—that the press failed to report that there was "overwhelming eyewitness testimony" that the shots came from behind a stone wall—is also sophistical. None of the hundred or so Warren Commission witnesses who testified on the matter or were questioned by the FBI said that they saw a rifle being fired from behind the stone wall. The *ear*witness testimony, which is undependable in determining the source of any shots where there is a possibility of echoes, was divided. More than half the witnesses thought the shots originated in some spot other than the Depository building, but only a few of the earwitnesses thought the shots came from the direction of the stone wall.[9] Moreover, the press *did* report that the majority of the earwitnesses thought the shots came from some place other than the Book Depository. In fact, this was reported by Walter Cronkite on the same CBS "News Inquiry" on which Garrison had himself appeared less than three weeks before he made these blanket charges of "news suppression" on NBC.[10]

## 5. The CIA Agent

Finally, the assertion that Oswald was a CIA agent, as has already been shown, was based on Garrison's own private interpretation of "missing" or classified documents that he had never seen. Of the five examples of "news suppression" that Garrison cited, then, not one was based on accurate information.

As a practicing district attorney, Garrison surely understood both the limits of so-called scientific evidence and its usefulness in impressing the general public. Nonetheless, he told a national television audience that the complex questions surrounding the assassination had long since been resolved by "scientific evidence" that proved Oswald innocent, but that the nation's press had not reported the existence of this evidence. Yet when it is examined, the "scientific evidence" he cites turns out to be either specious or misinterpreted, and the "news" that he claimed was "suppressed" is no more than a series of untruths.

# The Federal Establishment

> The federal government is a party with a special
> interest in this case. Our investigation has shown
> that the federal investigation was faked and the
> Warren Commission inquiry was faked to conceal
> the fact that President Kennedy was killed in a
> professionally executed ambush.
>
> —Jim Garrison, May 29, 1968, press release

Another of Garrison's sweeping charges about a "second
conspiracy" was that the federal government—through
its agents Lyndon Johnson, Robert Kennedy, J. Edgar
Hoover, Earl Warren, and Attorney General Ramsey
Clark—was involved in a sinister plot to quash his
investigation.[1] It would have been difficult to gain-
say Garrison's imputation of federal obstruction if he
had charged merely that the government was hinder-
ing his case. Certainly federal agencies were less than
co-operative, and important federal officials, including
Attorney General Clark, openly (and often harshly)
criticized the New Orleans investigation. But Garrison's allegations went far beyond the charge of
interference in this sense. He accused the federal government of conspiring to wreck his investigation specif-

ically because it harbored a motive of its own in concealing the truth about the assassination, and he leveled his accusation in no uncertain terms: ". . . the United States government—meaning the present administration, Lyndon Johnson's administration—is obstructing the investigation—any investigation. It has concealed the true facts—to be blunt about it—to protect the individuals involved in the assassination of John Kennedy."[2] In other words, he charged that the government knows the truth and, in concealing it, is itself conspiring to protect the conspirators.

So far, Garrison has offered only two specific items of "evidence" to support this charge. The first item is the previously discussed photograph of the assassination site showing a man with a closed fist—which by Garrison's surmise conceals the bullet that killed the President. From this conjecture he went on to postulate that the man in the photograph is a federal agent, that the bullet has been turned over to the federal government, and that the government consequently knows the assassin's identity.[3] The second item of evidence he mentions is a telegram that was supposedly sent to J. Edgar Hoover before the assassination. Garrison charged at a New Orleans news conference in December 1967 that this telegram, which he has been unable to obtain, proves that Oswald telephoned the Dallas field office of the FBI five days before the assassination and gave details of the plot, which were then forwarded by interbureau telegram to Hoover in Washington. This, Garrison claimed, was proof that President Johnson had "actively concealed evidence about the murder of his predecessor."[4] When a reporter asked him what evidence he had that such a telegram ever existed, he answered, "If you and I were in a closed room, I could prove it. But I'm not going to allow any evidence to get out now."[5] His evidence, he later revealed on the Johnny Carson show, was simply a story that Mark Lane had told him.[6]

Apart from such stories by Garrison and Lane, the charge of federal complicity is based almost solely on the fact that there *is* government secrecy. According to Garrison's logic, the government would not classify information pertinent to the assassination unless it had something to hide. Garrison has persistently exploited popular suspicions about secrecy, accusing those who would, in his estimation, benefit most from the maintenance of such secrecy. For example, after noting that part of the Warren Commission's documents are classified in the National Archives, Garrison claimed on a Texas television show in December 1967, "They destroyed evidence in every possible way. The President of the United States, the man who has the most to gain, the man who gained more than any other human from the assassination, is the man who issued the executive order concealing vital evidence for seventy-five years so that we can't look at it, so that you can't look at it, so that no American can see it for seventy-five years. Now, this was an executive order by Lyndon Johnson, the man who gained the most from the assassination."[7]

No such executive order has ever been issued. Many investigative files are withheld from use by law for seventy-five years—a number arbitrarily selected to exceed the life span of persons likely to be mentioned in the reports—in order to safeguard confidential information (such as tax returns), to protect confidential informers, and to avoid embarrassing innocent persons mentioned incidentally.[8] But in the case of the Warren Commission's documents, McGeorge Bundy, acting on behalf of President Johnson, sent a special request to the Archivist of the United States that the seventy-five year ban be waived wherever possible and that much of the material be opened to the public. Following guidelines approved by Bundy, all the agencies involved in the investigation were to review their files and declassify everything except pages containing the names of confidential informers, information damaging to innocent parties, and information about the agencies' operating procedures. There was to be a periodic review by all the agencies concerned.[9] By the time Garrison had begun his own investigation, virtually all the documents that could be declassified according to these guidelines had been opened to public scrutiny.[10] Garrison's claim in *Playboy* that "any document the CIA wanted classified was shunted into the Archives without examination by the sleeping beauties on the Commission" is simply untrue.[11] *All* the relevant documents relating to the inquiry which are now in the Archives were sent there by the Warren Commission after the Warren Report was published. Most of the CIA reports were prepared to answer specific questions put to the Agency by Commission lawyers, and there is no reason to assume that they went unread.

Garrison's tactic of claiming that the proof which supports his charges has been ensconced in classified documents is hardly an original one. For example, in

1950, Senator Joseph McCarthy asserted before the
Tydings Senate Sub-Committee that his celebrated
charge of eighty-one card-carrying Communists working in the State Department was supported by classified evidence in FBI files, and he vehemently de-
manded to know why the Truman administration was
keeping secret vital evidence that would show the ex-
tent of the Communist conspiracy in the State Department. Taking unprecedented action, President Truman
waived executive privilege and ordered the files made
available to the Tydings Committee. When it became
abundantly clear that these files were concealing no
evidence to support McCarthy's charges, the Senator
simply declared that the files had been "raped and
rifled" before they were shown to the Committee and
continued to demand that the "real files" be released.[12]
The government, McCarthy charged, was using its
powers of secrecy to conceal a gigantic conspiracy involving Communists and fellow travelers. In his campaign against the forces of secrecy, McCarthy also attacked the CIA as "the worst situation of all," and con-
sistently denounced the news media for abetting the
conspiracy by suppressing the "truth" and attacking
him.[13]

The distinguishing mark of the paranoid style,
Richard Hofstadter writes, is "the curious leap in imagination" between fact and fantasy which is made at some
critical point in an argument to cover a gap in reason-
ing.[14] Consider in this light the following remarks by
Garrison, taken from one of the many speeches he delivered during the fall of 1967.

Is this a Great Society which allows innocence to be butchered as Oswald was, with no concern, no interest? Which allows the guilty, the murderers to walk the streets, knowing without any question who they are, knowing what happened, is this a Great Society? Is it a Great Society which causes blackouts in news centers like New York when there's a development in the case? . . . Is this a Great Society which monitors your phone if it has the slightest bit of curiosity about you? This is not a Great Society—this is a Dangerous Society, a society which despite the lip service to Populism . . . is so morally threadbare that the futures of your children are in danger.[15]

Here "the curious leap in imagination" is made between the fact that some investigative files are still classified and the fantasy that the government is protecting the assassins by censoring the news, monitoring telephone calls, and threatening the futures of children. (It is worth noting, incidentally, that the image of "innocence . . . butchered as Oswald was" creates complications in the case of Clay Shaw, who was, after all, indicted for a conspiracy that involved Lee Harvey Oswald.)[16] In Garrison's case against the news media, a leap is made between the fact that the media failed to broadcast some *un*truths about the assassination and the fantasy of a conspiracy to suppress the news. In his charges against the CIA, a saltatory advance is made from missing or nonexistent evidence to the fantasy of CIA complicity in the assassination. Central to this tripartite conspiracy is the obsessive fascination with secrecy. For Garrison, the CIA epitomizes all that is feared in governmental secrecy: an invisible government, answerable to no one, with unlimited resources and unlimited power. Since all its acts are veiled in secrecy, it may be postulated to be the "secret force" behind any event. The suppression of news is for Garrison the means by which dark secrets are kept from the public, and the conspiracy maintained. The "clever manipulation of the mass media is," in Garrison's words, thus "creating a concentration camp of the mind."[17] The government, Garrison claims, "*is* the CIA and the Pentagon"—an elite that perpetuates its power by concealing the truth about the assassination.[18]

# 3

# Public Opinion

# The Torment of Secrecy

The people of this country do not have to be protected from the truth. This country was not built on the idea that a handful of nobles, whether located in our federal agencies in Washington, D.C., or in news agencies in New York, should decide what was good for the people to know and what they should not know. This is a totalitarian concept which presumes that the leaders of our federal government and the men in control of the powerful press media constitute a special elite which by virtue of their nobility and their brilliance empower them to think for the people.

—Jim Garrison, July 15, 1967, NBC-TV

As his investigation continued, Garrison appeared to become increasingly obsessed with governmental secrecy, and less directly concerned with the issues of his court case. His concern with secrecy became especially pronounced in his television appearances: he stated on New Orleans television, "The CIA has infinitely more power than the Gestapo and NKVD of Russia combined . . . we are blocked by this glass wall of this totalitarian, powerful agency which is worried about its power."[1] On Dallas television he said, "It did not occur to me that the President would have federal agencies conceal the truth from the people, it didn't occur to me that all these honorable men would conceal the truth from the people, that they would frame a man, Oswald, who had never fired a shot, and that they would knowingly protect the assassins."[2] On European television he asserted, "The President of the United States by executive order has taken all this critical evidence and has ordered that it be kept secret for seventy-five years, which means the lifetime of all living Americans. This has got to be the first time in history that the man who profited most from the murder has announced that evidence is going to be kept secret for seventy-five years. . . . I think that he can't be allowed to make the decision that the American people can't see this evidence, it is just an unbelievable situation and he should not be allowed to get away with it."[3] And on the Johnny Carson show, he said, "An element of the Central Intelligence Agency of our country killed John Kennedy and the present administration is concealing the facts . . ." and then went on to say, "The honor of this country is at stake, and if we don't do something about this fraud, we will not survive, and there is no way to survive if we don't bring out the truth about how our President was killed four years ago."[4] On another television program, Garrison explained that he was "trying to get the word out that something is wrong, that they killed John Kennedy and that the next President of the United States that tries to slow down the warfare machine and tries to bring this country to the brink of peace, will be assassinated too. There is no question about it. They will just do it in a different way, a different town, perhaps it will be an accident the next time or another Communist, but he will be assassinated because this juggernaut is self-sustaining, dedicated to a perpetual cold war and it will not tolerate anybody trying to stop it."[5]

In *The Torment of Secrecy*, a trenchant analysis of the sociological background of the excesses which accompanied the investigations of Senator McCarthy and others in the nineteen-fifties, Edward Shils traces the public's fascination with conspiracy and subversion—which helped sustain the inquisitions for the better part of a decade—to a deeper fear of secrecy that has persisted in American political culture since the Revolution. This fear of secrecy is reflected in the demand that all areas of political life be opened to public scrutiny, and the suspicion that any enclave of government or special-interest group that veils its activities in secrecy is harboring a conspiratorial elite. The concern with secrecy becomes pathological, Professor Shils argues, when secrets in and of themselves are considered to be subversive of society and the legitimate boundaries of privacy are transgressed in pursuit of them. Particularly vulnerable to the fear and fascination of secrecy are the alienated and the extremist; Shils explains:

> The ideological extremists—all extremists are inevitably ideological—because of their isolation from the world, feel menaced by unknown dangers. The paranoic tendencies which are closely associated with their apocalyptic and aggressive outlook make them think that the ordinary world, from which their devotion to the ideal cuts them off, is not normal at all; they think that it is a realm of secret machinations. What goes on

in the world of pluralistic politics, in civil society, is a secret to them. It is a secret which they must unmask by vigorous publicity. Their image of the "world" as a realm of evil, against which they must defend themselves, and which they must ultimately conquer, forces them to think of the enemy's knowledge as secret knowledge.[6]

Garrison's appeal runs along very similar lines. Implicit in his charges is the suggestion that a special elite, by concealing from the populace the truth about the assassination, has appropriated to itself political control of a nation. Power is maintained through such secret machinations as "thought control," "blackouts in news centers," the "manipulation of the mass media," and the monitoring of telephone calls. The struggle for the possession of vital secrets about the assassination is depicted in apocalyptic terms. A "military-industrial juggernaut," as he said on Dutch television, which is "committed to a land war in Asia with or without hydrogen bombs" will lead the nation to a disastrous war unless the secret of the assassination can be wrested from this elite. Society is described as being so "morally threadbare that the futures of your children are in danger," a society on the verge of becoming "a concentration camp of the mind."[7] Since the leaders of the political world, including President Johnson, Chief Justice Warren, and Attorney General Clark, were held to be actively assisting the conspiracy by suppressing the true facts of the case, salvation depended, in this view, not on a political process, but on exposing the secrets by which the elite maintains its power.

Whether Garrison has been exploiter or victim of

"the torment of secrecy" is problematic; in either case, his relentless agitation against governmental secrecy apparently succeeded, if the barrage of mail his office received after each of his public appearances was any measure, in stimulating a good deal of public concern. After the District Attorney appeared on Johnny Carson's show, for example, and cited a list of classified CIA documents which he said "are secret until the year 2039," and then charged that an element of the CIA had assassinated President Kennedy "and the present administration is concealing the facts,"[8] his office received an estimated two hundred to three hundred letters a day for more than a week after the television broadcast.[9] Thomas Bethell, who read through the daily correspondence for Garrison's staff, found that the vast majority of the letters sent directly to Garrison's office showed primary concern with the notion that the government and the news media were systematically withholding facts about the assassination, and the question that most seemed to occupy the incensed letter-writers was, according to Bethell, "Why is so much information classified secret if there is nothing to hide?"[10] The same themes of secrecy and suppression ran paramount in the mail that *Playboy* received after the interview with Garrison appeared in the October 1967 issue. The responses, which one editor described as "an exceptionally large number even for *Playboy*," were almost ninety per cent favorable to Garrison, but here again the writers of the letters were, characteristically, concerned less with discussing the facts of the assassination than with denouncing governmental secrecy and news suppression. Typical were such comments as: "It is now up to the American people to force President Johnson to open the National Archives"; "What really amazes me is the fact that such people as Governor Rhodes of Ohio and the President, who could open the files in the National Archives for investigation, choose to sit on this vital information"; "Even the Kennedy assassination fades into insignificance against the more important issues. Whether there was actual or incidental collaboration between mass media and government agencies, whether dishonesty, corruption, lying, and secrecy pervade the government as strongly as Mr. Garrison insists . . . the web [of suppression] has reached into the sacred depths of our national institutions."[11] To be sure, such mail is not a representative sample of opinion, and at best only indicates that the fear of secrecy can be tapped in those most easily aroused to respond—those who write letters.

Yet, if the public-opinion surveys administered by Louis Harris and Associates are an accurate gauge, a very considerable portion of the population as a whole appeared to have been persuaded by Garrison's claims. Early in 1967, before the New Orleans investigation became public knowledge, a Harris poll indicated that some forty-four per cent of the American people thought that the murder of President Kennedy was the result of a conspiracy.[12] In May 1967, shortly after Garrison had announced the discovery of a plot, had gone on to arrest Clay Shaw, and had charged the CIA with concealing evidence, a survey by Harris indicated that sixty-six per cent of the American public now believed that the assassination had been carried out by a conspiracy.[13] A third Harris survey, taken in September, revealed that despite the fact that Garrison's inquiry had produced no tangible results, sixty per cent of the people still believed that Kennedy had been killed by a conspiracy.[14] To be sure, it is by no means clear that Garrison was chiefly responsible for effecting this remarkable change in public opinion. It can be argued that a considerable number of people are naturally disposed to make a conspiratorial interpretation of any event as historically momentous as the assassination of a President. Indeed, earlier Harris surveys showed that at least thirty per cent of the population believed from the outset that Oswald had not acted entirely alone, and continued to believe this after the Warren Commission rendered its verdict.[15] Moreover, Harris concluded from the questionnaires filled out by his respondents immediately after the Warren Report was issued that eleven per cent of the population may be considered "chronic doubters who tend to feel that the 'real' story about almost any important public event is never quite told."[16] The fact that there was a marked increase—from thirty-one per cent to forty-four, according to Harris surveys—in the number of people who believed in a conspiracy when the Warren Commission became the subject of heated controversy, owing to the publication in 1966 of a number of books and articles criticizing the Report, may reflect a certain resistance by the general public against accepting a purported "truth" that is neither clear-cut nor obviously irrefutable. The idea that even a few points in the Warren Report were subject to dispute, or that even a few of its facts could be differently interpreted, probably led many people to reject, or at least doubt, the over-all conclusion that the Commission had put forward so emphatically.

In any event, the change in public opinion seems to have been substantial after Garrison appeared on the scene. Between February and May of 1967, Harris surveys indicated nearly half (sixteen out of thirty-five per cent, to be exact) of the people who had believed that Oswald was the lone assassin were now changing their minds. In other words, once Garrison began issuing his charges some thirty million Americans who had apparently been neither predisposed to believe in a conspiracy nor moved by earlier criticism of the Warren Report started having second thoughts on the question of a lone assassin.

In presenting to the public his own conclusions about the assassination of President Kennedy, Garrison enjoyed some strong advantages over all other critics of the Warren Commission. The first and most obvious is simply the authority of his office. As the district attorney of a major American city, Garrison was able to make news at will, merely by submitting charges, issuing subpoenas, and making arrests. Moreover, to many people it must seem almost inconceivable that an elected prosecutor's carefully worded "factual" statements—for example, that "At 12:45 P.M. on November 22, the Dallas police had broadcast a wanted bulletin for Oswald"—could be demonstrably false.

The District Attorney's claim to being an expert on forensic matters made it somewhat difficult, for those accepting that claim, to reject his authoritative-sounding pronouncements on evidence. When Garrison explained on national television how "scientific tests" had exonerated Oswald, few members of the audience were in a position to know that the "evidence" and the "tests" he described with such positive assurances were, in fact, spurious.[17] This imputed expertness on evidentiary matters also gave Garrison an advantage over those who attempted to dispute his statements. For example, when Johnny Carson attempted on his show to refute Garrison's contention that no identifiable prints were found on the rifle used in the assassination, by pointing out that Oswald's palmprint was in fact found on the rifle, Garrison replied authoritatively, "The palmprint was not confirmed by the federal government either,"[18] despite the fact that the palmprint was positively identified as Oswald's by three fingerprint experts, Sebastian Latona and Ronald G. Wittmus of the FBI, and Arthur Mandella of the New York City Police Department—and then further confirmed by the FBI laboratory as having come from Oswald's rifle.[19]

Still another important benefit that Garrison derived from being a public prosecutor with a case pending was the right to refuse to divulge the evidence on which his charges were based. And Garrison exercised his right on virtually all his radio and television interviews. Pressed for the basis of his allegations, he would reply, as he did on the Johnny Carson show, "I am not allowed, as an attorney, to come up with evidence until the case comes to trial."[20] He also utilized this prerogative to make his evidence against Clay Shaw appear firmer than in fact it was, particularly in the *Playboy* interview. Take, for example, his statement that "we know from incontrovertible evidence in our possession who the real Clay Bertrand is—and we will prove it in court."[21] Since Garrison charged that Clay Shaw used the alias of Clay Bertrand, this is an extremely important claim, but although the question of the identity of Clay Bertrand was a central issue in the perjury trial of Dean Andrews, which took place well after the *Playboy* interview was conducted, Garrison failed to introduce any evidence at that time concerning it. Later, a source in Garrison's office suggested that the evidence to which Garrison had been referring in the *Playboy* interview was a library card taken out under the name Clay Bertrand and bearing Clay Shaw's former business address.[22] This card hardly qualifies as incontrovertible evidence. For one thing, the card turned up well after Shaw was arrested, and, for some reason, bore no date of issuance or expiration. For another, the signature on the card was definitely not in Clay Shaw's hand—a fact that Garrison's own staff confirmed.[23] In other words, it appears that someone other than Clay Shaw filled out a library card under the alias that Garrison claimed Shaw used and put Shaw's former business address on it.*

Garrison also enjoyed the advantage of what might be called strategic plausibility. As Hannah Arendt points out in her essay "Truth and Politics," the liar is usually more persuasive than the truthteller, simply because he can fashion his facts to meet his audience's

---

* The affair is discussed at some length by William Turner in the "official history" of the case in the January 1968 issue of *Ramparts*. Turner, however, does not divulge the fact that the signature on the card is not Shaw's.

expectations.[24] Since Garrison is under no compulsion to reveal his evidence, there is nothing to prevent him from contriving his own explanation of the assassination. Whereas neither the Warren Commission nor its critics could offer a definite motive for the murder of the President, Garrison can. He states categorically in *Playboy*, "President Kennedy was killed for one reason: because he was working for a reconciliation with the U.S.S.R. and Castro's Cuba." And he goes on to declare that this is not mere speculation, insisting, ". . . we know enough about the key individuals involved in the conspiracy—Latins and Americans alike—to know that this was their motive for the murder of John Kennedy."[25]

To those who expect a momentous event to have some significant cause, Garrison's explanation naturally sounds more logical than the explanation that a lone assassin acted out of personal disaffection.

# XI

# The Making of a Demagogue

If the press has any doubts about me, if they think
I'm politically ambitious, if they really think I'd
charge somebody for some kind of personal gain,
then they should raise the question. That's fine.
Because I'll survive. . . .

—Jim Garrison speaking before the Radio
and Television News Association of
Southern California, November 1967

A demagogue can survive only so long as the mass
media take him seriously enough to print his charges
and give him exposure. The relation is not, however,
entirely one-sided. The demagogue, free of any con-
straint of veracity, is always in a position to provide
journalists with the kinds of exclusive stories and
sensational charges which stimulate widespread interest—and circulation. The way in which Garrison's
case developed, from the abrupt arrest and pre-trial
hearing of Clay Shaw to the constantly changing
configuration of assassins and conspirators, is perhaps
more closely connected to Garrison's struggle to obtain
access to the news media than it is to his evidentiary
investigation.

*Life*

Garrison decided to investigate the assassination of President Kennedy, it will be remembered, in November 1966 after he discussed the matter with Senator Russell Long on a plane flight to New York City. Shortly after he returned to New Orleans, the District Attorney informed David Chandler, *Life*'s man in New Orleans, of his plans. He also suggested that *Life*, which had itself just called for a new inquiry into the assassination in a cover story entitled "A Matter of Reasonable Doubt,"[1] might be interested in "a joint investigation."[2] Chandler relayed the offer to the New York office, and Richard Billings, then an associate editor for special events, was promptly dispatched to New Orleans. On December 7, Garrison met with Billings and Chandler and offered to give *Life* reporters complete and exclusive access to his investigation. All he asked in return was that *Life* assist him in investigating matters outside his jurisdiction.[3] Billings agreed to what he termed "an exchange of information," and for the next ten weeks *Life* photographers and reporters became an integral part of the District Attorney's investigation: interviewing witnesses, photographing interrogation sessions, attending staff conferences, and preparing a major story on Garrison's prime suspect, David Ferrie.[4] However, relations became somewhat troubled after Ferrie's sudden death in late February 1967 and, a week later, Garrison arrested a new suspect, Clay Shaw. Garrison later told me that he had been promised a cover story in *Life* if he made an arrest, and when it failed to materialize he realized that *Life* "had knuckled under to White House pressure."[5] Billings categorically denied that any such commitment was ever made by representatives of *Life*.[6] Chandler said that Garrison assumed from the amount of interest *Life* had manifested that an arrest would lead to a cover story, but no promises were ever made.[7]

There were a number of reasons why *Life* never published the extensive story it had prepared on the Garrison investigation. Immediately after Shaw was arrested, Chandler, who had been present at the "brainstorming sessions" in which Garrison speculated that Clay Shaw might be the elusive Clay Bertrand, informed senior editors at *Life* that he now thought the entire investigation might be a publicity stunt.[8] Billings also had some doubts after the arrest of Shaw: he had been present when Assistant District Attorney Sciambra gave Garrison an oral report of Perry Raymond Russo's story, and, at this time, it contained nothing about a "conspiracy" or about a "Bertrand" who fitted the description of Shaw.[9] The publication of James Phelan's story on Garrison in the *Saturday Evening Post* was probably the final straw. Garrison, apparently disappointed over *Life*'s failure to publish, not only had granted Phelan a long interview in Las Vegas, but had also allowed him to examine the documents. And so Phelan found the memorandum from Sciambra which revealed that Russo's original story was very different from the one he had told in court—and although Garrison and Sciambra publicly denied this, Billings was in a position to know that it was true, and

*Life* after this quickly lost interest in the Garrison affair.[10]

## Playboy

Garrison next sought exposure in *Playboy*, agreeing to allow the magazine to publish an extensive interview about his investigation *before* the case came to trial. The editor in charge of the project estimated that the interview, which contained allegations ranging from CIA involvement in the assassination to the arrival of Fascism in America, represented "$1,605,000 worth of editorial space," although it is not clear whether he is referring to the publicity which the interview would gain for *Playboy* or for Garrison.[11] There is no reason to assume, however, that the decision to publish the interview was based primarily on mercenary considerations; for, in giving Garrison "the chance to present his side of the case" before the trial took place,[12] *Playboy* was, after all, acting in the well-established tradition of American journalism which holds that every story has two sides—and that what is controversial is news. This concept of news does not necessarily require that an account, so long as it fairly represents one side of a story, be factually accurate. In recommending the interview for publication, one senior editor thus wrote:

> Garrison comes off as sincere, eloquent, even brilliant. *But even if he were a nut*—and I don't think it's possible for anyone to read this and come away with that conclusion—I would still want to run this, just because

it is the first complete reconstruction of the assassination events as seen through Garrison's eyes. At worst, if Garrison is totally repudiated (in light of the facts he presents this seems highly unlikely), we have an interview in the Shelton-Rockwell genre. At best, if he is vindicated, then we perform a genuine public service, almost in the Pulitzer prize category.[13] [Italics in the original memorandum.]

A second editor's evaluation ran along similar lines:

Garrison is revealed as an intelligent, hearty, and ballsy guy—certainly not a kook—with a credible case, even if he turns out wrong. He indicts everyone from the CIA, to Warren's Commission, to N.B.C. (he gets a bit gratuitous there and dissipates his venom), and he probably is somewhat paranoid, but I think anyone would be who was conducting a non-Establishment investigation into the assassination.[14]

In a memorandum to Hugh M. Hefner, the publisher, Murray Fisher, a senior editor, summed up the reasons for publishing the interview:

Even if he's wrong (which is possible), even if he's insincere (which I doubt), even if the accusations about his impropriety are true (which seems not to be the case), Shaw is still going to go to trial in October [1967] and the interview (coming out two or three weeks before it begins) will be very big news.[15]

Since the interview would be "big news" whether Garrison was right or wrong, there existed little incentive to check out the factual accuracy of the piece before publication. (Almost all of Garrison's references to the testimony in the Warren Commission's volumes,

which for the most part could have been checked
without a great deal of effort, were either incorrect or
misleading. For example, in purporting to quote from
a Supplementary Investigation Report which appeared
in Volume XIX of the Warren Commission's testimony,
Garrison simply altered the words in the text from "I
advised him" to "I was advised" to make his point.)[16]
Despite the prediction of A. C. Spectorsky, the associate
publisher, that the interview would lead to twenty-
four libel suits,[17] it was rushed to publication in
September to anticipate a trial that did not materialize.
And although *Playboy* may not have realized the expected $1,605,000 in free publicity, Garrison did his
share by appearing on radio and television shows in
New York and California in conjunction with the publication of the interview. In *Playboy*, the New Orleans
District Attorney found (as he put it in one of the
television appearances) "an opportunity to try and
communicate some of the issues in the case" to a
national audience.[18]

## The Anti-Establishment Press

Moreover, Garrison found allies, eager to proselytize
on his behalf, among dissident political writers who
consider themselves part of what they call "the anti-
Establishment press." His charge that there was a conspiracy between the government and the mass media
to conceal the truth from the people accords perfectly,
after all, with what such journals see as their *raison
d'être*. It is therefore hardly surprising to find his
speeches printed verbatim in such papers as the *Los*

*Angeles Free Press*, and to find his portrait on the cover of *Ramparts*, with the words:

> Who appointed Ramsey Clark, who has done his best to torpedo the investigation of the case? Who controls the CIA? Who controls the FBI? Who controls the Archives where this evidence is locked up for so long that it is unlikely that there is anybody in this room who will be alive when it is released? This is really your property and the property of the people of this country. Who has the arrogance and the brass to prevent the people from seeing that evidence? Who indeed? The one man who has profited most from the assassination—your friendly President, Lyndon Johnson![19]

Garrison thus finally obtained the cover story that *Life*, despite his efforts, had denied him.

Anti-establishmentarianism tends to make strange bedfellows. Among Garrison's most ardent supporters was the *Councilor*, the bimonthly official journal of the Citizens' Council of Louisiana, which claims a circulation of some two hundred and sixty thousand, and which actively campaigns against Communism, the suppression of news by the mass media (supposedly controlled by Zionist interests), race mongrelization (a plot aided by the CIA and the Rothschilds), and the insidious intrusion of federal authority into the sacred domain of states' rights. That Garrison had been "fought by Sterns, Newhouse papers, and Agnes Meyer" (i.e., the NBC affiliate in New Orleans, WDSU-TV; the *Times-Picayune* and *States-Item*; and the *Washington Post* and *Newsweek*) was for the *Councilor* sufficient reason to lend Garrison its enthusiastic support.[20] The logic of *Ramparts* has not been significantly different; William Turner concluded one of his articles on Garrison in the magazine by saying that the anti-Garrison tactics of NBC, *Newsweek,* and the daily press "smack of desperation—and indicate that there is much to hide."[21] The *Councilor* went along with most of the details of the plot theory outlined in *Ramparts,* differing only in its belief that it was "the left wing of the CIA," not the right wing, and that New York Communists, rather than right-wing extremists, were behind the conspiracy.[22] (Perry Russo told the *Councilor* in an exclusive interview that David Ferrie was really a "Marxist" and follower of Che Guevara.)[23]

### The New York Review

Garrison's cause also found champions in more highly respected journals that pride themselves on their intellectual credentials—notably the *New York Review of Books,* which rejected the Warren Commission's conclusions because the Commission's investigation was defective but embraced Garrison's investigation despite its far more glaring defects. Professor Richard Popkin, in a lengthy defense of Garrison's investigation in the *New York Review,* argues that Garrison should be given a "fair hearing" in court, and not have his case "prejudged" by the press. He claims that while Garrison has "studiously avoided any discussion of Shaw and the specific evidence against him," the press has interviewed "potential witnesses," evaluated the evidence, made "charges against the District Attorney and his office . . . in effect, trying the case out of court." The "wave of attacks in the press and TV" against Garrison, Popkin contends, "surely prejudices a fair trial." He concludes that no investigation of Garrison is necessary, for "if the evidence is as contrived and cockeyed as the press and TV allege, they should expect that twelve jurors along with [the judge] will see through it."[24] It is true that the right of a defendant not to be prejudged is a fundamental principle of jurisprudence. And pretrial publicity, by prejudicing public opinion, can certainly deny the defendant his right to a fair hearing. Jim Garrison, however, is *not* the defendant. Clay Shaw is! The rights of the defendant have been established precisely to counterbalance the powers of the state. Popkin's plea that the press suspend scrutiny and criticism of Garrison's methods would, if it were taken to heart, undermine a defendant's legitimate protection against the possibility of a prosecutor's using his power and resources to fabricate evidence and intimidate witnesses. Moreover, Popkin's contention that Garrison "studiously avoided" discussing the evidence seems disingenuous, at best. The fact is that an interview that Popkin had with Perry Russo was arranged by the District Attorney himself.[25] It was Garrison, too, who told reporters that he had found Jack Ruby's coded telephone number in both Shaw's and Oswald's address books, and repeated the allegation on television and to newspaper reporters even after it was shown to be false.[26] It was Garrison who stated in the *National Observer*, "There is no way that Clay Shaw can get an acquittal."[27] It was Garrison who allowed Mark Lane and William Turner to photostat evidence in his files. And it was Garrison who, in his *Playboy* interview and on his subsequent coast-to-coast tour, made numerous references either to evidence in the Shaw case or to Shaw himself (including the demonstrable falsehood that Shaw was with President Kennedy "on an airplane flight in 1963").[28] Indeed, Garrison went on about the case in speeches, radio talk shows, television programs, press conferences, and interviews almost without pause. Of course, most of the evidence Garrison discussed is spurious, but surely that makes it all the more imperative for the press not to waive its responsibility for examining it closely.

Popkin's way of dismissing the charges leveled against Garrison is similarly cavalier. He chides the *New York Times* for accepting at face value, and printing on its front page, the allegations made against Garrison by the convicted burglar John Cancler; Popkin points out that when the grand jury later questioned Cancler about the accusations, he invoked the Fifth Amendment. The fact that Cancler exercised his Constitutional right to protect himself against self-incrimination, Popkin concludes, affects the "credibility" of his charges.[29] Yet, does this necessarily follow? Cancler had charged that his fellow prisoner, Vernon Bundy, confided to him that he was going to give perjured testimony at Clay Shaw's preliminary hearing, testimony that would inculpate Shaw.[30] If this is true, Cancler was an accessory before the fact in the perjury, and might indeed have incriminated himself by admitting this to the grand jury. Besides, the mere fact that Cancler took the Fifth Amendment, though it may have signaled a want of courage on his part, surely cannot be said to affect in itself the man's credibility (although there were those among the followers of the late Senator Joe McCarthy who insisted that it did).

Popkin's notion that there is no need for the press to scrutinize Garrison's techniques for recruiting witnesses and assembling evidence because if the evidence is contrived a judge and jury will see through it and "destroy Garrison at the trial" shows an unusual confidence in the legal process. While it is true that a judge and jury can detect contradictions in testimony and other incongruous evidence, there is no certainty at all that they can uncover perjury that has been systematically arranged for, with one perjurer corroborating another's testimony, or that they can recognize artfully fabricated "facts" purposely designed to fit into the pattern of evidence. Exposure of such systematic fraud would, in fact, depend on an outside investigation of the prosecutor's means and methods. Gene Roberts, of *The New York Times*, and Walter Sheridan, of NBC, have stated that in separate inquiries they discovered at least six witnesses who said that they had been offered bribes, blackmailed, or otherwise coerced by Garrison's representatives.[31] All were, in one way or another, vulnerable people. William Gurvich said that while he was working for Garrison he saw the way the powers of a district attorney's office could be used "to intimidate and coerce witnesses."[32] Popkin intimates that Sheridan and Gurvich may have had some ulterior motive in revealing information about Garrison's mode of operation.[33] One can, as the British philosopher A. J. Ayer points out, always sustain one's beliefs in the face of apparently hostile evidence if one is prepared to make the necessary *ad hoc* assumptions, and in this case supporters of Garrison seem all too ready to assume that everyone who criticizes Garrison's conduct is part of a plot to conceal the truth. But such rationalization explains nothing. During the time I studied Garrison's investigation and had access to his office, the only evidence I saw or heard about that could connect Clay Shaw with the assassination was fraudulent—some devised by Garrison himself and some cynically culled from criminals or the emotionally unstable. To fail to report this information so that Garrison might have a "fair hearing" in court could preclude the possibility of the defendant's ever receiving *his* fair hearing in court.

To see the issue of the assassination as of such overwhelming importance that the juridical rights of the defendant may be neglected, the Constitutional rights of witnesses disdained, the scrutiny and criticism of the press suspended, and the traditional methods of the state's prosecution ignored is to accept a curious sort of situational ethics. It is to say that in a search for facts the means can be disregarded if the ends—the facts—are of enough consequence. Fred Powledge, writing in the *New Republic*, suggests the dilemma: "I had the irrational feeling that he [Garrison] was on to something. I had the equally startling feeling that it did not really matter if Garrison were paranoid, opportunistic, flamboyant, or if his witnesses were not candidates for *The Defenders*. Was he *right?*"[34] But can the process of establishing the truth ever be separated from its end product—the truth? Facts must be selected, interpreted, and arranged in the context provided by other information before they take on meaning. Factual evidence can be established as truth, as Hannah Arendt points out, only "through testimony by eyewitnesses—notoriously unreliable—and by records, documents, and monuments, all of which can be suspected as forgeries."[35] If one has reason to doubt the process by which "facts" have been ascertained or confirmed, how can one ever be certain that they bear any relation to the truth, or even that the "facts" themselves are not outright fabrications? For data can be accepted as factual truth if, and only if, the probity of the investigator is also accepted. A demagogue who demonstrates a willingness to alter elements of a story when it serves his purpose may temporarily excite public opinion, but he can never establish his version of the event as the truth.

In view of the shortcomings of the Warren Commission's investigation, it becomes apparent that there is no easy way to devise a process for ultimately answering such complex and elusive historical questions as those provoked by the assassination of President Kennedy. Indeed, there can be no certainty that such a process is even within our institutional means. But there *can* be certainty that as long as the means by which an investigation has been conducted remain suspect the truth will never be fully established.

# Notes

## Prologue: Oswald in New Orleans

1. *Hearings before the President's Commission on the Assassination of President Kennedy*, Washington, D.C., 1964 (hereinafter *Hearings*), Vol. I, p. 18.
2. *Hearings*, Vol. III, pp. 59–60.
3. *Report of the President's Commission on the Assassination of President Kennedy*, Washington, D.C., 1964 (hereinafter *Report*), p. 726.
4. *Hearings*, Vol. II, pp. 468–71.
5. *Report*, p. 727, and *Hearings*, Vol. II, p. 517, also Commission Exhibit 1117, and *Hearings*, Vol. X, p. 271.
6. Commission Exhibit 408.
7. *Hearings*, Vol. I, pp. 68, 85.
8. *Hearings*, Vol. XI, p. 331, pp. 326–39 *passim.*
9. Commission Exhibit 93. Oswald's erratic spelling has been corrected and the punctuation regularized.
10. *Hearings*, Vol. XX, pp. 512–21.
11. Commission Document 75, U.S. National Archives, and Commission Exhibits 1413, 1414, 3119.
12. Commission Document 75.
13. *Hearings*, Vol. XX, pp. 512–21.
14. *Hearings*, Vol. X, p. 90.
15. *Hearings*, Vol. V, p. 401.
16. *Hearings*, Vol. I, p. 25.
17. *Hearings*, Vol. XXVI, p. 771.
18. *Hearings*, Vol. I, p. 64.
19. *Hearings*, Vol. XX, p. 525.
20. *Hearings*, Vol. XX, p. 524.
21. *Report*, p. 533.
22. *Hearings*, Vol. X, pp. 33–34, 82–83.
23. *Hearings*, Vol. X, p. 35.
24. *Hearings*, Vol. X, pp. 35–38.
25. *Hearings*, Vol. X, p. 54.
26. *Hearings*, Vol. IV, pp. 436*ff.*
27. *Hearings*, Vol. XX, p. 529.
28. *Hearings*, Vol. XXI, p. 621.
29. *Hearings*, Vol. XXI, pp. 634*ff.*
30. *Hearings*, Vol. XI, p. 171.
31. *Hearings*, Vol. XX, pp. 529–30.
32. *Hearings*, Vol. XX, pp. 263–64.
33. *Report*, p. 412.
34. *Hearings*, Vol. I, p. 24.
35. *Hearings*, Vol. I, p. 22.
36. *Hearings*, Vol. I, p. 22.
37. *Hearings*, Vol. XI, p. 372.
38. *Report*, pp. 413*ff.*, and *Hearings*, Vol. XXIV, p. 590, also *Report*, p. 734.
39. *Hearings*, Vol. I, p. 50.

## I. The Prosecutor

1. *New Orleans Times-Picayune,* February 25, 1967.
2. Edward Jay Epstein, *Inquest: The Warren Commission and the Establishment of Truth,* New York, The Viking Press, 1966.
3. *Ibid.,* p. 103.
4. *Hearings,* Vol. XXII, pp. 826–27.
5. *Hearings,* Vol. XXVI, p. 771.
6. *Hearings,* Vol. XXII, p. 826.
7. For an example of this conflict, see Epstein, *op. cit.,* pp. 31–42.
8. Fred Powledge, "Is Garrison Faking?" *New Republic,* June 17, 1967, p. 16, and James R. Phelan, "The Vice Man Cometh," *Saturday Evening Post,* June 8, 1963, pp. 67–71.
9. A. J. Liebling, *The Earl of Louisiana,* New York, Simon and Schuster, 1961, pp. 83–84.
10. Allan P. Sindler, *Huey Long's Louisiana,* Baltimore, Johns Hopkins Press, 1968, pp. 94–116, and V. O. Key, Jr., *Southern Politics,* New York, Vintage, 1949, pp. 156*ff.*
11. Phelan, *op. cit.,* pp. 67–71.
12. Garrison *v.* Louisiana, 379 U.S. 64 (1964).
13. *Times-Picayune,* April 13, 1967.
14. *Ibid.,* March 3, 1967, and Edward Weggman (counsel for Clay Shaw), interview with author (hereinafter Weggman Interview).
15. *Ibid.,* April 4, 1967.
16. *Ibid.,* May 13, 1967.
17. *Ibid.*
18. "The JFK Conspiracy: The Case of Jim Garrison," NBC–TV, June 19, 1967 (hereinafter "JFK Conspiracy," NBC–TV). The original interview with Garrison took place on WDSU–TV, New Orleans, an NBC affiliate.
19. *Times-Picayune,* May 18, 1967.
20. "JFK Conspiracy," NBC–TV.
21. "JFK Conspiracy," NBC–TV.
22. Jim Garrison, interview with author (hereinafter Garrison Interview).
23. *Los Angeles Free Press,* November 17, 1967. A similar statement was also made by Garrison on "Page One," WABC–TV, New York, September 24, 1967.

## II. The Suspect

1. James A. Autry, "The Garrison Investigation: How and Why It Began," *New Orleans,* April 1967, p. 8.
2. Garrison Interview.
3. William W. Turner, "The Garrison Commission on the Assassination of President Kennedy," *Ramparts,* January 1968, p. 52.
4. Fred Powledge, *op. cit.,* p. 14.
5. Harold Weisberg, *Oswald in New Orleans: A Case of Conspiracy with the CIA,* Canyon Books, 1967, p. 395.

6. Richard H. Popkin, "Garrison's Case," *New York Review of Books*, September 14, 1967, p. 28.
7. Rosemary James and Jack Wardlaw, *Plot or Politics*, New Orleans, Pelican, 1967, p. 72.
8. *Hearings*, Vol. VIII, p. 14, Vol. XXII, pp. 826–27.
9. Popkin, *op. cit.*,
10. James and Wardlaw, *op. cit.*, pp. 42–43.
11. *Ibid.*, p. 45.
12. *Ibid.*
13. *Ibid.*, p. 46.
14. *Ibid.*
15. Garrison Interview.
16. James and Wardlaw, *op. cit.*, p. 45.
17. *Times-Picayune*, February 27, 1967. Also quoted in Secret Service Report (Control No. 620), National Archives.
18. Thomas Bethell, interview with author (hereinafter Bethell Interview).
19. Secret Service Report quoted in Weisberg, *op. cit.*, p. 180.
20. Garrison Interview, and *New York World Journal Tribune*, March 5, 1967.
21. James and Wardlaw, *op. cit.*, p. 49.
22. Garrison Interview.
23. *Ibid.*
24. *Hearings*, Vol. XI, pp. 334, 337.
25. Andrew J. Sciambra, interview with author (hereinafter Sciambra Interview).
26. Garrison Interview.
27. David L. Chandler, interview with author (hereinafter Chandler Interview).
28. Richard N. Billings, "Garrison and the JFK Plot," *Long Island Press*, May 15, 1968.
29. Chandler Interview, and *Times-Picayune*, June 28, 1967.
30. Garrison Interview.
31. *Times-Picayune*, April 25, 1967.
32. Letter from Gordon Novel.
33. James and Wardlaw, *op. cit.*, p. 34.
34. *Ibid.*, pp. 38–39.
35. Richard N. Billings, "Garrison Convinced of Plot," *Miami Herald*, May 22, 1968, and interview with author (hereinafter Billings Interview).
36. *Times-Picayune*, February 26, 1967, and James and Wardlaw, *op. cit.*, p. 41.
37. *Ibid.*, February 23, 1967.
38. *Ibid.*, February 26, 1967.
39. Billings Interview.
40. *Times-Picayune*, June 28, 1967.
41. Transcript of Preliminary Hearing, Russo Testimony, p. 188.
42. *Ibid.*, pp. 182–83, 206.
43. Sciambra Memorandum. (Author's files.)
44. Billings Interview.

45. *Ibid.*
46. James R. Phelan, interview with author (hereinafter Phelan Interview).
47. Billings Interview, and Sciambra Interview.
48. *New York Times,* March 14, 1967.

## III. The Witnesses

1. *"Playboy* Interview: Jim Garrison," *Playboy,* October 1967 (hereinafter *Playboy*), p. 62.
2. *Ibid.*
3. *Times-Picayune,* March 15, 1967.
4. *Ibid.*
5. Transcript of proceedings in connection with Preliminary Hearing, Clay L. Shaw, Arrestee (hereinafter *Transcript*), pp. 227*ff.,* 212–14.
6. *Transcript,* p. 208.
7. *Transcript,* p. 279–80.
8. *Transcript,* p. 192.
9. *Transcript,* pp. 231–32.
10. *Transcript,* p. 203.
11. *Transcript,* p. 204.
12. *Transcript,* p. 246.
13. *Transcript,* p. 114.
14. William H. Gurvich, interview with author (hereinafter Gurvich Interview).
15. *Times-Picayune,* March 18, 1967.
16. *Ibid.,* March 23, 1967.
17. James R. Phelan, "Rush to Judgment in New Orleans," *Saturday Evening Post,* May 6, 1967, pp. 21–25.
18. *Ibid.*
19. Sciambra Memorandum.
20. Billings Interview, and *supra,* Chapter III.
21. *Report,* pp. 726–30.
22. "JFK Conspiracy," NBC–TV (statements of Ruth Paine and Mrs. Jesse Garner).
23. *Report,* pp. 730–38.
24. "JFK Conspiracy," NBC–TV.
25. Boston *Globe,* March 28, 1967.
26. Phelan, "Rush to Judgment in New Orleans," *op. cit.*
27. Sciambra Memorandum.
28. *Ibid.*
29. *Ibid.*
30. "JFK Conspiracy," NBC–TV.
31. *Playboy,* p. 62.
32. "JFK Conspiracy," NBC–TV.
33. Phelan Interview.
34. *Times-Picayune,* June 21, 1967.
35. "JFK Conspiracy," NBC–TV, and *New York Times,* June 12, 1967.

36. *New York Times,* August 14, 1967, and *Times-Picayune,* April 13, 1967.
37. *Times-Picayune,* August 13, 1967.
38. *Los Angeles Free Press,* November 17, 1967 (transcript of speech by Garrison).
39. *Times-Picayune,* August 13, 1967.
40. Bethell Interview.
41. Official Clerk's Records for the Criminal District Court for the Parish of Orleans, "State of Louisiana *v.* Clay L. Shaw," and Supplemental Memorandum.
43. *New York Times,* February 14, 1968.
44. *New York Times,* May 29, 1968, and U.S. District Court, Eastern District of Louisiana, "Clay L. Shaw *v.* Jim Garrison," Civil Action 68–1063, Section B.
45. *New York Times,* August 14, 1968.
46. Weggman Interview, and Garrison in *Los Angeles Free Press,* August 23, 1968.
47. *New York Times,* December 10 and 12, 1968.

## IV. The Search

1. Bethell Interview.
2. Garrison Interview.
3. Letter from Bethell to author.
4. Bethell Interview.
5. *New York Times,* December 11, 1967.
6. Garrison Interview, and *New York World Journal Tribune,* March 5, 1967.
7. Garrison Interview, and *Times-Picayune,* July 12, 1968.
8. *Times-Picayune,* May 24, 1967, also Part III, CBS–TV News, June 27, 1967, and Garrison interviewed by Boy Jones, WWL–TV. New Orleans, May 21, 1967.
9. *Playboy,* p. 165.
10. James D. Squires, "Cuban Guerrilla Team Killed JFK, Garrison Thinks," *Nashville Tennesseean,* June 22, 1967.
11. *Playboy,* p. 170.
12. Bethell Interview.
13. "Page One," WABC–TV, New York, September 24, 1967 (hereinafter "Page One").
14. *Times-Picayune,* April 8, 1967.
15. "Page One."
16. *Ibid.,* and *Playboy, passim.*
17. "Page One."
18. *Ibid.*
19. *Playboy,* p. 159.
20. "Page One."
21. "Tonight" Show, NBC–TV, January 31, 1968.
22. *Playboy,* p. 162, and *Times-Picayune,* September 22, 1967.

23. "Joe Dolan Talk Back" Program, KNEW, Oakland, California, September 15, 1967.
24. "Face to Face with Murphy Martin," WFAA–TV, Dallas, Texas, December 9, 1967.
25. Bethell Interview.
26. "Face to Face with Murphy Martin," *op. cit.*
27. *Ibid.*
28. *Times-Picayune,* July 13, 1968.
29. *Playboy,* p. 166.
30. *Ibid.,* and *Berkeley Barb,* September 15–21, 1967.
31. FBI Report, June 11, 1964, Commission *Report* 1245; also, letter from Bethell.
32. Bethell Interview.
33. *Playboy,* p. 166.
34. "Tonight" Show, *op. cit.*
35. Bethell Interview, and Turner, *Ramparts, op. cit.*
36. *Playboy,* p. 160.
37. Letter from Bethell.
38. Garrison Interview, and Turner, *Ramparts, op. cit.*
39. *Playboy,* p. 163, and Bethell Interview.
40. Letter from Bethell.
41. Eric Norden, interview with author.
42. "Gordon Novel, Plaintiff, *v.* Jim Garrison and HMH Publishing Co., Inc., a Delaware Corporation, Defendants." Case No. 67 C 1895, in the United States District Court for the Northern District of Illinois, Eastern Division (hereinafter *Playboy File*). Exhibit B.
43. Bethell Interview.
44. James D. Squires, *op. cit.*
45. Bethell Interview. (Also, Garrison allowed author to read Johnson's statement.)
46. Bethell Interview. Also Statement of Cedric Younger Von Rolleston, Oneda P. Von Rolleston, July 17, 1967. Author's files.
47. Affidavit of Oneda P. Von Rolleston and Cedric Younger Von Rolleston, March 16, 1968. Author's files.
48. *Times-Picayune,* June 28, 1967.
49. *Playboy,* pp. 167–68.
50. Bethell Interview.
51. *New York Times,* November 9, 1968.
52. *Chicago Tribune,* December 30, 1967.

## V. The Thousand-Pound Canary

1. Ramond Moley, *Politics and Criminal Prosecution,* Minton, Balch & Co., 1929, p. 50, and *passim.*
2. *New York Times,* June 12, 1967.
3. *Ibid.*
4. "JFK Conspiracy," NBC–TV.
5. "JFK Conspiracy," NBC–TV.

6. Hugh Aynesworth, "The JFK Conspiracy," *Newsweek*, May 15, 1967.
7. *Playboy*, p. 64.
8. *Ibid.*
9. Gurvich Interview.
10. *Ibid.*
11. Dean Andrews, interview, June 1967, and Interviews taped for NBC News with Andrews, October 1967 (hereinafter Andrews Interviews).
12. Andrews Interviews.
13. *Ibid.*
14. *Ibid.*
15. *Ibid.*
16. *Ibid.*
17. *Ibid.*
18. *Times-Picayune*, April 13, 1967.
19. Andrews Interviews.
20. *Ibid.*
21. *Supra*, Chapter III.
22. Memorandum by David Lifton concerning Kerry Thornley (hereinafter Lifton Memorandum).
23. *Ibid.*
24. *Ibid.*
25. *Ibid.*, and *Miami Herald*, February 1, 1968.
26. Bethell Interview, and Letter from Harold Weisberg to Fred Newcomb.
27. Lifton Memorandum.

## VI. The Tangled Web

1. Richard H. Rovere, *Senator Joe McCarthy*, New York, Meridian, 1964, p. 140.
2. The speech is reprinted in its entirety in *The Los Angeles Free Press*, December 22–28, 1967.
3. Edward A. Shils, *The Torment of Secrecy*, New York, The Free Press, 1956, pp. 24–25, and *passim*.
4. *Saturday Evening Post*, May 6, 1967, pp. 22–25.
5. *New Orleans States-Item*, April 25, 1967, and Rosemary James, interview with author.
6. *Newsweek*, May 15, 1967, pp. 36–40.
7. Martin Waldron, "Some Say It's Garrison Who's in Wonderland," *New York Times*, May 14, 1967, and Jack Wardlaw, interview with author.
8. *Times-Picayune*, May 9, 1967.
9. *New York Times*, May 10, 1967.
10. *Times-Picayune*, May 10, 1967.
11. *Infra*, Chapter VII.
12. *Chicago Tribune*, December 30, 1967, and Stephen White, *Should We Now Believe the Warren Report?*, New York, Macmillan, 1968, p. 276.

13. *Times-Picayune,* May 22, 1967. (The interview was carried on WWL–TV, New Orleans, May 21, 1967.)
14. "JFK Conspiracy," NBC–TV.
15. Epstein, *op. cit.,* pp. 98–100.
16. *Times-Picayune,* June 20, 1967.
17. *Times-Picayune,* June 21, 1967, and unpublished portion of transcript of *Playboy* interview.
18. "Statement by Jim Garrison," NBC–TV, July 15, 1967.
19. *Playboy,* p. 108.
20. *New York Times,* July 17, 1967.
21. *Times-Picayune,* July 19, 1967.
22. *New Orleans States-Item,* June 23, 1967.
23. White, *op. cit.,* pp. 274–75 (see note 12).
24. *Times-Picayune,* June 27, 1967.
25. *Times-Picayune,* June 24, 1967.
26. *Playboy,* p. 68.
27. "Page One."
28. "Warren Foresees Trial News Curbs," *New York Times,* September 5, 1967.
29. "Garrison Assails Tokyo Words of Chief Justice," *Times-Picayune,* September 5, 1967.
30. *Ibid.*
31. Billings Interview.
32. "Witness in Assassination Plot Hints at Cuban Link," *New York Times,* April 4, 1967.
33. "Novel Will Be Returned—Ohio," *Times-Picayune,* May 10, 1967.
34. Bethell Interview.
35. "Ohio Frees 'Witness' Sought by Garrison," *New York Times,* July 4, 1967.
36. *Playboy,* p. 172.
37. *Los Angeles Free Press,* November 17, 1967.
38. *Times-Picayune,* July 12, 1968.
39. *Time,* August 2, 1968, p. 56.
40. *Times-Picayune,* July 12, 1968.
41. *Ibid.*

## VII. The CIA

1. Richard Hofstadter, *The Paranoid Style in American Politics and Other Essays,* New York, Vintage, 1967, p. 4.
2. "Issues and Answers," ABC–TV, May 28, 1967.
3. Martin Waldron, "Garrison Charges CIA and FBI Conceal Evidence on Oswald," *New York Times,* May 10, 1967.
4. *Times-Picayune,* May 18, 1967.
5. "Garrison Says CIA Knows the Slayers," *New York Times,* May 23, 1967, and *Times-Picayune,* May 22, 1967.
6. *Times-Picayune,* May 24, 1967, and Associated Press Interview with Garrison by Laura Foreman, May 23, 1967.

7. *Los Angeles Free Press,* November 17, 1967.
8. "Tonight" Show, *op. cit.*
9. Transcript of Interview with Dutch television, Reel 1, p. 2.
10. *Playboy,* pp. 70, 72, 74, 160.
11. *Times-Picayune,* May 7, 1967, and *Playboy,* p. 70.
12. Epstein, *op. cit.,* pp. 93–94.
13. Garrison Interview.
14. *Playboy,* p. 74.
15. Interview with James B. Rhodes, Deputy Archivist, U.S. National Archives (hereinafter Rhodes Interview).
16. Wesley J. Liebeler, interview with author.
17. *Playboy,* p. 74.
18. *Los Angeles Free Press,* December 22, 1967.
19. *Playboy,* pp. 167–68.
20. Josiah Thompson, *Six Seconds in Dallas,* New York, Bernard Geis Associates, 1967, p. 217, and Billings Interview.
21. *Playboy,* p. 72.
22. *Los Angeles Free Press,* November 17, 1967.
23. *Hearings,* Vol. XVIII, p. 188.
24. *Los Angeles Free Press,* November 17, 1967.
25. *Playboy,* p. 70, and Garrison Interview.
26. Commission Document 75, FBI File 89–69.
27. Garrison Interview.
28. *Report,* pp. 697–98.
29. *Supra,* Chapter IV.
30. *Playboy,* p. 70.
31. *Ibid.*
32. Interview with Fred Freed, producer of "JFK Conspiracy," NBC–TV.

## VIII. The Media

1. Jim Garrison, "With Liberty and Justice for All," foreword to Harold Weisberg, *op. cit.,* p. 13.
2. "Statement by Jim Garrison," NBC–TV, July 15, 1967.
3. *Hearings,* Vol. IV, p. 22.
4. *Hearings,* Vol. IV, p. 24.
5. *Report,* p. 123, and Commission Exhibit 2637.
6. *Report,* pp. 560–62.
7. *Hearings,* Vol. III, p. 494.
8. *Report,* p. 152.
9. Josiah Thompson, *op. cit.,* pp. 254–70.
10. Stephen White, *op. cit.,* p. 248, and Transcript of CBS–TV News "Inquiry," Part II, June 26, 1967.

## IX. The Federal Establishment

1. *Los Angeles Free Press,* November 17, 1967 (text of speech by Garrison).

2. "Face to Face with Murphy Martin," WFAA–TV, Dallas, Texas, December 9, 1967, and *supra*, Chapter **IV**.
3. "Garrison Says Oswald Gave FBI a Tip Before Assassination," *New York Times*, December 27, 1967.
4. *Ibid.*
5. *Ibid.*
6. "Tonight" Show, NBC–TV, January 31, 1968.
7. "Face to Face with Murphy Martin," *op. cit.*
8. Rhodes Interview.
9. *Ibid.*, and letter from McGeorge Bundy. Author's files.
10. *Ibid.*
11. *Playboy*, p. 72.
12. Richard H. Rovere, *op. cit.*, pp. 148–50.
13. *Ibid.*, pp. 47–48, and "McCarthy: A Documented Record," *The Progressive*, April 1954, pp. 59–63 and *passim*.
14. Richard Hofstadter, *op. cit.*
15. *Los Angeles Free Press*, November 17, 1967.
16. The indictment reads, "Clay L. Shaw . . . did willfully and unlawfully conspire with David W. Ferrie, herein named but not charged, *and Lee Harvey Oswald,* herein named but not charged, and others, not herein named, to murder John F. Kennedy" (italics mine), *Times-Picayune*, March 23, 1967.
17. *Playboy*, p. 178.
18. *Ibid.*

## X. The Torment of Secrecy

1. Garrison Interview, WWL–TV, New Orleans, May 21, 1967.
2. "Face to Face with Murphy Martin," *op. cit.*
3. Garrison on Dutch television, reel 2.
4. "Tonight" Show, NBC–TV, January 31, 1968.
5. Garrison on Dutch television.
6. Edward A. Shils, *op. cit.*, pp. 234, 37–47 and *passim*.
7. See p. 138, *supra*.
8. "Tonight" Show, *op. cit.*
9. Bethell Interview.
10. *Ibid.*
11. Synopsis of letters received by *Playboy* (author's file).
12. *Washington Post*, March 6, 1967.
13. *Washington Post*, May 29, 1967.
14. *News and Observer*, Raleigh, N.C., September 20, 1967.
15. *Washington Post*, October 19, 1964.
16. *Washington Post*, October 19, 1964.
17. *Supra*, Chapter **VIII**.
18. "Tonight" Show, *op. cit.*
19. *Report*, pp. 123–24.
20. "Tonight" Show, *op. cit.*
21. *Playboy*, p. 66.
22. Bethell Interview.
23. *Ibid.*

24. Hannah Arendt, *Between Past and Future*, New York, Viking Compass Edition, 1968, pp. 250–51.
25. *Playboy*, pp. 74, 157.

## XI. The Making of a Demagogue

1. "A Matter of Reasonable Doubt," *Life*, November 25, 1966, pp. 38–53.
2. Chandler Interview.
3. *Ibid.*, and Billings Interview.
4. Billings Interview.
5. Garrison Interview.
6. Billings Interview.
7. Chandler Interview.
8. *Ibid.*
9. Billings Interview, and *infra*, Chapters II, III.
10. Billings Interview.
11. *Playboy* File, Exhibit II–1.
12. *Playboy*, p. 62.
13. *Playboy* File, July 20, 1967, Memorandum, Exhibit E.
14. *Playboy* File, July 19, 1967, Memorandum, Exhibit D.
15. *Playboy* File, Exhibit C–1.
16. *Playboy*, p. 162. Cf. *Hearings*, Vol. XIX, p. 534.
17. *Playboy* File, Exhibit II–1.
18. "Page One."
19. *Ramparts*, January 1968, front cover.
20. *The Councilor*, Shreveport, Louisiana, June 1, 1967.
21. William Turner, "The Press Versus Garrison," *Ramparts* August 1968, p. 12.
22. *The Councilor*, May 12, 1967. Cf. *Ramparts*, January 1968, p. 2.
23. *The Councilor*, "Russo Says: David W. Ferrie Was a Marxist," June 15, 1967.
24. Richard H. Popkin, "Garrison's Case," *New York Review of Books*, September 14, 1967, p. 20.
25. *Ibid.*, p. 25.
26. *Infra*, Chapter I. Cf. *Playboy*, p. 174, and cf. Garrison Interview, "Issues and Answers," ABC–TV, May 28, 1967.
27. Jerrold D. Footlick, "Jim, Do You Really Believe All This Stuff?" *National Observer*, January 22, 1968, p. 1.
28. *Playboy*, p. 162.
29. Popkin, *op. cit.*, p. 21.
30. *New York Times*, June 12, 1967.
31. The witnesses were John Cancler, Miguel Torres, Sandra Moffit, Fred Lemanns, Alvin Beauboeuf, Dean Andrews.
32. Gurvich Interview.
33. Popkin, *op. cit.*, p. 23.
34. Fred Powledge, *op. cit.*, p. 18.
35. Hannah Arendt, *op. cit.*, p. 243.

# Index